# TRAINING
# THE WORKING
# LABRADOR

# TRAINING
# THE WORKING
# LABRADOR

The Complete Guide to Management and Training

## JEREMY HUNT

STACKPOLE
BOOKS

Copyright © 2013 Jeremy Hunt

First published in North America in 2013 by
STACKPOLE BOOKS
5067 Ritter Road
Mechanicsburg, PA 17055
www.stackpolebooks.com

A catalogue record for this book is available from the Library of Congress

ISBN 978-0-8117-1319-1

Design and typesetting by Paul Saunders

**Photographs**
All photographs are the copyright of the author unless credited otherwise

Frontispiece photo, page 2: Peter Bates.
Photo opposite Chapter One, page 6: Anne Taylor

Printed in China

# Contents

# CHAPTER ONE

•

# The Breed Explained

THE LABRADOR RETRIEVER – versatile, adaptable, intelligent, dependable. No wonder it's the UK's most popular dog with Kennel Club puppy registrations regularly exceeding 36,000 a year. It has been the top breed in America for the last 18 years with 154,000 dogs registered in 2012 with the American Kennel Club. The breed's many virtues have justifiably earned the Labrador world-wide acclaim as it continues to fulfil an ever-increasing variety of roles far beyond that of its primary job as a working gundog.

The breed has a remarkable ability to learn, acquit itself with a range of skills and respond to a host of different training regimes. Combined with its unflappable temperament and biddability, the popularity of the Labrador will forever endure.

The Labrador is certainly a supreme shooting dog but the breed's easy-going attitude has guaranteed its unassailable position as the most popular dog with UK families looking for an easily managed companion. The Labrador has long been the iconic image of the Guide Dogs and fulfils an exemplary role working in detection services and with search and rescue teams in countries across the world.

But inevitably over the years the breed has undergone change. No breed of dog remains the same in terms of how it looks and to some extent how it behaves. Within the world of Labrador breeding a marked degree of

Fenway Brock –
a good-looking
working Labrador
*(Photo: Trafford)*

polarisation has been driven by the requirements of dogs to fulfil their role as working gundogs or those destined for the show ring. This divergence has not only impacted on the appearance of these two 'types' of Labrador; selective breeding by the two factions within the breed – working and showing – has led to many show-bred Labradors losing their natural ability to work and many working Labradors no longer looking like typical examples of the breed.

Similarly there is equal disparity in the way working ability is perceived. Some show-bred dogs are trained by their owners to produce an acceptable level of skill as working gundogs. But however good their standards may be they rarely meet those required by the upper echelons of the working Labrador fraternity who have higher expectations in terms of speed, style, drive and hunting ability.

Not all working-bred Labradors are paragons of virtue in the shooting field. Many owners of shooting dogs tolerate shortcomings in their dog's

working ability – quite often because the dog hasn't received the training necessary to match its potential.

So within one breed we have show-bred Labradors and we have a leaner, more athletic and active type bred primarily for work as a gundog. While this book is aimed at those who own, or are about to own, a working Labrador with the primary objective of training the dog for shooting, picking-up or to compete at tests or field trials, it's important to recognise the large population of working-bred Labradors living as pets or companions. These dogs would undoubtedly greatly enjoy learning the basic skills of a working gundog so I hope this book inspires those who own a working Labrador purely as a companion.

By embarking upon appropriate basic training these intelligent dogs can go some way to fulfilling the purpose for which they were bred. And in so doing help alleviate the boredom and frustration that's so often the root cause of the hyperactivity and behavioural problems seen in working Labradors living in a domestic 'non working' environment.

A bitch combining show and working breeding proving her skill as a shooting dog
(Photo: Anne Taylor)

While buying a Labrador that's going to become a working gundog means choosing a puppy or dog of the appropriate breeding, it isn't always quite as straightforward as some may assume. There's certainly nothing quite so appealing as a Labrador pup, but it's important not to get smitten by the first litter you look at. There are careful considerations to make based on information of which many prospective owners aren't always aware.

To present a fair picture of the Labrador in all its guises it's necessary to understand the origins of this remarkable breed and how it has become so popular. Of Canadian descent we are certain, but it was a black dog seen retrieving sticks out of Poole harbour in Dorset almost 200 years ago that triggered the first imports. The dog in question had seemingly arrived on a fishing boat from Newfoundland and was seen retrieving by the 2nd Earl of Malmesbury. Impressed by its skills in water the Earl was prompted to buy the dog for the shooting on his estate. Its success as a gundog led to more dogs of similar type being imported to the UK but it was the 3rd Earl of Malmesbury who actually decided to start breeding these dogs – and he called them 'Labradors'.

The Kennel Club recognises the Labrador as a gundog and, as for all breeds, it has a blueprint. This is known as the 'breed standard' and lays down the desired appearance of each breed in terms of physical construction and other relevant traits including movement and temperament. This standard is the one to which those who breed Labradors for the show ring must adhere if they want to win awards because it is the standard upon which all dog show judges base their deliberations.

But the 'breed standard' in itself creates a major problem for the Labrador. In the other 210 breeds recognised by the Kennel Club – for instance breeds as diverse as Poodles or Afghan Hounds or Chihuahuas – there is a breed standard which is the benchmark. Breeders keep the best pups for themselves to continue their breeding programme for the show ring and sell the rest as pets.

But while there remains only one 'breed standard' for the Labrador, the type of dogs it inevitably encourages breeders to produce for the show ring has no bearing on those bred for work. The Labrador, despite having a Kennel Club 'breed standard', is not a single breed in terms of uniformity in looks and certainly not in purpose. There is no doubt that the Labrador *per se* performs all its various roles extremely well – be that as an accomplished field trial dog, a working gundog, a show dog, a detection dog or a family companion. But why are there such considerable variations in the way the breed looks and how and why have they occurred?

Given that the modern Labrador is the result of a wide divergence of genetics used by breeders to produce dogs to fulfil an equally wide range of specific roles, the genetics responsible for producing dogs to satisfy the breed's primary function as a working gundog are separate from those used

The working Labrador is the most popular dual-purpose gundog *(Photo: Peter Bates)*

to produce Labradors for the show-ring. This division within the breed produces two distinct types as a consequence.

Show-bred and working-bred Labradors are most easily identified by their differing appearance. In essence the trend has been to breed working Labradors that are more athletic in their construction compared with those bred for the show-ring. But we live in a world of extremes and while there may now be the first signs of change as breeders on both sides of the divide seek 'moderation', the last 40 years have seen many show-bred Labradors become heavier and less active and working Labradors become lighter in their conformation and more 'racey' in appearance. Yes, some breeders in both camps have sought not to follow these extremes – be they show breeders or working breeders – but in general no one can deny that today we have one Labrador breed that has become two.

'Horses for courses' many say and they may well be right. In the show-ring there are some outstanding examples of the breed – or should I say out-standing examples of Labradors that fit the Kennel Club's 'breed standard'. While even the most staunch working enthusiast would be hard-pressed not to admire some of the top winners in the show ring, they are neverthe-less very different from the dogs we see in the shooting field.

Ironically, despite everything that show-breeders have sought to achieve in their dogs over the last 40 years, many still relish comments from a judge such as 'looks like he could do a day's work.' In the most extreme cases some show-bred Labradors have developed heads akin to those of Rott-weilers with a 'heavy' physical construction that's totally alien to a working gundog and with movement that impedes the active locomotion required to sustain a dog during a day in the shooting field.

Among the working ranks it's still possible to find dogs that are un-deniably Labradors in appearance, but sadly there are vast numbers that are not. The 'black whippet' syndrome – the term so often used to describe the lighter-framed, working black Labrador – is still very prevalent and it's sad to hear first-time owners assume that such is the norm and is acceptable.

So why have so many Labradors bred for work lost the breed's true characteristics? The focus of attention on working ability, game-finding, speed, style and drive has been prioritised by those aiming to produce Lab-radors able to win awards in the increasingly competitive world of field trials. Good looks don't win field trials and while there is sound reasoning behind why brains and ability are paramount in dogs involved in successful competitive gundog work, it's a shame the prioritisation of these traits has come at such a high price in terms of the way many working Labradors look today.

So the last 40 years have seen the appearance – or to give it the correct term 'conformation' – of many working Labradors change dramatically as selection for desired traits has focussed almost totally on ability. Even today many who work their dogs believe conformation isn't of paramount importance, even though it makes the Labrador what it is. Although this attitude has been responsible for the appearance of many of today's working Labradors, the trend has caused working Labradors to forfeit more than their aesthetic appeal.

Fenway Lincoln after a successful day's shooting in Victoria, Australia (*Photo: Darren Wilkie*)

A lot of working Labradors have narrow heads which is usually referred to as a 'snipey' look. It often comes with a 'hard' eye which is totally alien to a breed whose head and expression is very much its trademark. Lightly-boned limbs and an athletic physical construction produced for speed have very much become the norm in working Labradors. But ironically there are some very important functional traits that are still vitally important to working Labradors and yet have been lost – despite the fact that they are still highly desirable in the show-ring.

Show judges still look for the true double-coat that provides the ultimate weatherproofing for the breed and ensures a dog is well insulated from the cold and prevents water from permeating through to the skin. Similarly a show-ring judge will look closely at a dog's tail to see if it has the breed's distinctive otter tail – an invaluable aid to swimming, balance and forward propulsion in water when retrieving.

Both of these breed characteristics are functional traits that are essential for a working Labrador to do its job effectively. I well remember many years ago buying a pup from a top winning field trial kennel. As it matured it was clearly going to have a very thin coat and an equally thin tail. As a working dog she was outstanding, but on a wet winter day's shooting she quickly became soaked to the skin and shivered miserably. She was fearless in water but it was disturbing to see her struggle when trying to use her ineffective 'rudder' to help her during a retrieve from a river. That dousing also meant she remained cold and wet for the rest of the day's work. In my opinion thin-coated Labradors are not only ill-equipped for the job, they also spend a lot of time being cold. That means they burn up more energy and are harder to keep in the correct body condition during the shooting season.

It's understandable that dogs capable of winning top awards at field trials – and achieving all the kudos that such success brings – don't have to be good looking. No field trial judge has ever awarded marks for good looks! Over the years the most garlanded field trial winners have been regarded as the benchmark for excellence among those breeding working Labradors and many outstanding dogs have had a hugely beneficial impact on working bloodlines. But these haven't necessarily been good looking Labradors and their lack of 'breed type' has been perpetuated – almost considered a 'fair exchange' for superior working ability.

There's no doubt that other breeds have occasionally found their way into the genetic make-up of today's working Labrador. For those with a wider experience of gundogs and aware of the tell-tale signs, it isn't difficult to spot glimpses of past infusions. Clear hints of English Pointer, English Springer Spaniel or Greyhound – to name just a few – can be identified in certain dogs even to this day. Such alliances were surreptitiously undertaken with the sole purpose of introducing traits from other breeds that were perceived to be capable of enhancing ability in the working Labrador in some way – usually improved scenting and speed.

It's a shame that many working Labradors have been allowed to degenerate in their appearance over recent decades and while ability as a working gundog must remain a high priority, the 'machine' that was originally bred to perform this function must not be lost in the process – otherwise what is the point of having a Labrador in the first place. There are, nevertheless, breeders who have tried to adhere to a functional, effective but good looking working Labrador that combines ability in the field and yet is still

Anne Taylor's Ch Fabracken Remember Me – a top show winning bitch that picks-up regularly throughout the shooting season
*(Photo: Anne Taylor)*

undoubtedly typical of the breed. This 'type' of Labrador is often referred to as 'dual purpose', although in its truest sense this term denotes dogs that are good enough to work and be shown.

There is still a handful of breeders who not only work and compete with their dogs at field trials and tests but also show them. They are very much in the minority and their breeding policies seek to combine good looking working bloodlines with show-breeding genetics of the less extreme type. All credit to them for their efforts. These committed supporters of the Labrador breed don't always receive the respect they deserve, mainly because they fall into the 'middle ground'.

Show dogs that win at the highest level and attain the title 'Show Champion' can then go on to qualify for the Kennel Club's show gundog working certificate. If successful they then become a full 'Champion' – a status that denotes they have proved their basic working ability.

For a dog to achieve the holy grail of 'Dual Champion' status it must become a Show Champion and also a Field Trial champion but most would agree this title is now almost impossible to achieve. The last Labrador to carry this title was Dual Champion Knaith Banjo in 1946.

There are no field trial kennels that venture into the show ring – apart from where special classes for field trial or working dogs are scheduled. Breeders who are maintaining the working ability of their predominantly show-bred dogs are being brave enough, in some cases, to bring working bloodlines into their breeding programme. While it's very doubtful anyone involved in breeding field trial Labradors would consider using a show-bred dog, a handful of kennels breeding working Labradors – not necessarily focussed on competing at field trials – have, in the past, occasionally used dogs of less-extreme show 'type' that have included a good mix of 'middle ground' genetics from bloodlines that are also worked or used for picking up.

So there is some blending of show and working bloodlines but it's very peripheral and when one considers the popularity of the breed it is, in truth, an extremely small percentage. However we are starting to see more attention being paid to the appearance of working Labradors. While ability will always be the main driver in any breeding decision, there is an ever growing demand for good looking working Labradors – and some breeders are responding to that.

So the pool of Labrador genetics is certainly a very wide one considering this is one breed. The biggest challenge for anyone venturing into the world of working Labradors for the first time is gaining a clear under-standing of this diversity to help make the right decision about buying a pup or a young dog. Looking across the breed as a whole we can divide the Labrador into several categories – all as a result of the genetics of each.

Within Labradors that make up the working population of the breed it's often a surprise to many to find a considerable amount of divergence. Field trials are the system by which excellence in working ability is assessed. It's intensely competitive and produces, by wins in open trials, dogs and bitches good enough to carry the title of Field Trial Champion. Dogs and bitches of a wide range of 'working' breeding can attain the highest level of achievement in field trials as has been proved consistently over many years. Top field trial winners can have a pedigree rich in bloodlines of astound-ing merit or they may come from a more humble background of work-ing genetics and yet achieve greatness. But it's fair to say that more than a smattering of well proven genetics based on competitive gundog work of a high calibre occurs in the pedigrees of most Field Trial Champions.

While those involved in field trials tend to sustain their breeding pro-grammes with infusions of genetics from bloodlines with equally high standards of competitive success, many rank and file owners of working Labrador bitches turn to Field Trial Champion dogs when seeking a suitable sire for a litter. While some of these bitches will be well-bred, others may be less so. There is an assumption – and it's a valid one up to a point – that a top-winning field trial dog put to a bitch of relatively ordinary working breeding, will produce 'the goods'. As in any breeding venture, sometimes it works and sometimes it doesn't. So there is a wide swathe of working Labrador genetics from which many puppy buyers source their future working Labrador that is actually based on superior sires and mediocre bitches.

Field trials are judged and marks awarded based on each dog's perform-ance. While they remain the sole means of assessing working gundogs competitively in order to achieve champion status, the system does have its critics. Some field trial dogs are kept solely for competition and aren't used for shooting or picking-up. This has led to concerns about the true value of wins at field trials and whether or not they reflect a dog's actual work-ing ability or simply reflect its ability to perform within the parameters of competition. Opinions have also been expressed over the years concerning the stamina of some field trial dogs whose short 'blasts' of work on the trial

field do not always give an indication of how a dog can perform over a full day in the shooting field or cope with more taxing demands on his ability and stamina.

Whatever conclusions are reached by individuals concerning these issues, field trials remain the 'clearing house' for working Labradors seeking to climb the stairway to the stars and the genetics of most of those that become successful will continue to play a major part in the continued development of our working Labradors of the future.

And there is yet another strata of working Labradors – those that can best be described as 'parochial' and have remained relatively untouched by wider genetic influence. Quite often referred to as 'keeper bred', this is not simply a term that defines the person responsible for breeding them. In the wider context it often refers to a particular strain that may have been developed by an individual shooting estate or even by keepers and pickers-up in a localised area where a type of Labrador best suited to the particular

Ricky Maloney's FT Ch Tasco Monk of Mansengreen – a good looking top winning field trial dog (*Photo: Sharon Rogers*)

OPPOSITE PAGE Working Labradors are true athletes (*Photo: Sharon Rogers*)

terrain or work, has evolved. These strains can be interesting to observe. Sometimes they may be of a smaller type or even a larger type, perhaps stronger and more robust in conformation or even lighter and more racey. However they have been developed, and whatever traits have been concentrated upon, the primary aim has been to produce dogs most suited to the specific type of work asked of them.

Labradors bred for the show-ring have to be included in this overview. Most breeders and exhibitors of show-bred Labradors don't have any interest in the working ability of the breed and base all their breeding decisions on appearance and conformation in accordance with the breed standard. But as we have already acknowledged there are some purely show-bred dogs that are successfully used throughout the shooting season for picking up, others that work well as peg-dogs and an encouraging number that are taking part in tests and trials.

The Kennel Club's 'Working Gundog Certificate' (WGC) is open to all Kennel Club registered gundogs and their handlers. This isn't a competitive award but aims to show that dog and handler can work in a competent partnership and demonstrate the qualities needed to work on a shoot. It is also popular among the band of show exhibitors who like to confirm their dog's ability to work.

The Kennel Club's 'Show Gundog Working Certificate' was introduced to provide credible proof of the natural working ability of a Kennel Club registered gundog that had already proved it meets the breed standard by a qualification in the show ring. So a Labrador that has won a Challenge Certificate or previously qualified for Crufts through a breed class may be entered for a Show Gundog Working Certificate. The assessment is always held at a field trial or at a Show Gundog Working Day under a minimum of two judges of which at least one must be a Kennel Club 'A' Panel judge.

Among winners of the title of 'Show Champion' and who have upgraded to 'Champion' status there have been one or two surprises over the years among dogs that have been big winners in the ring but have then responded well to training and successfully claimed their show gundog working certificate.

There are also breeders who are primarily most active in the show-ring, but to fully enjoy the breed as a working gundog follow lines of breeding that produce a less-extreme type of show dog which retains a degree of natural working ability. Some of these breeders are highly successful in the show ring and achieve recognition from judges who prefer this type of Labrador.

Very few owners of show-bred bitches mate them to dogs that are totally of field trial breeding – although it's not unheard of. While in theory it would seem that such an alliance would combine to produce the 'best of both worlds', genetics aren't always quite so accommodating. The Labrador that looks like a top show winner but has the brains of a Field Trial Champion is the ultimate goal but the combination of two such diverse lines of breeding often serves to dilute the best from both sides and mediocrity can ensue in the progeny.

However that's not always the outcome and there are exceptions where this blending is working very successfully. Perhaps if we see more prepared to undertake this type of mating someone may hit the jackpot because there's no doubt some impressive dogs from a combination of show and working bloodlines are beginning to make their presence felt in the shooting field – and even competitively at novice and open stake level.

We began by discussing the fact that the Labrador, in the opinion of the Kennel Club, is one breed. I believe we have now quite clearly revealed that it certainly isn't. But despite this divergence the Kennel Club will register any litter of pups whose sire and dam is similarly registered. The Kennel Club does not make any assessment of the 'type' of Labradors it registers so pups produced from a mating of two dogs that may be Labrador in name only are readily accepted for registration. What is even more concerning, but perhaps not the place to be fully discussed here, is that the Kennel Club continues to register pups from parents that have undergone no health testing. So to buy a pup that is registered by the Kennel Club tells you only one thing – that the sire and dam are also registered. It discloses nothing about how a pup will look when it's mature and gives no indication about the health test (hips, elbows, eyes) results of the parents. It's important to understand that the Kennel Club registration can offer no guarantee about a pup other than the fact that it has two registered parents.

So it's essential to have a full understanding of the status of the breed in the UK and to be aware of the wide range of breeding combinations that can create what may well be termed a 'working Labrador'. Such a dog can look and perform across the full gamut of ability – hopeless or brilliant – and it can look every inch a Labrador or anything but a Labrador. And no information about any of those traits can be gleaned from its Kennel

Club registered status which, in all truth are just names and numbers on a certificate. While I firmly believe it's important to buy a pup from Kennel Club registered parents and that pups produced from matings of registered stock should also be registered, Kennel Club registration is simply that and nothing more.

Black Labradors are the most popular colour among those who work their dogs, although yellows have strong supporters. Fashions are ever-changing and a spate of successful yellow stud dogs or when major field trial awards are accounted for by yellows, can quickly lead to more of that colour emerging in the field and in competition. It's fair to say that black predominates the genetics of working Labradors but yellow now has a wide range of variations. There are yellow Labradors with deep yellow coats and there are others that are even verging on white. Fashion has certainly favoured the fox-red coat colour which in its truest form is a very deep red and not simply a deeper yellow. There appears to be no other reason for the increased demand for fox-red Labradors other than a 'fad'. The chocolate issue among working ranks has long been debated and while Labradors of this colour – which can vary from pale milk chocolate to dark brown – don't have a good reputation as working dogs, I have to say there is good reason for that, even though it's a rather unfair criticism.

The chocolate Labrador – and it would have been more appropriate if it had retained its original colour description of 'liver' – could not have been designed any better as the 'must have' among buyers of pet Labrador pups. Its popularity created a situation that still exists – one of mass production of pups whose breeding is based purely on colour. Chocolate Labrador pups offered for sale – and some have found themselves in working homes by default – have been mainly produced by individuals who feel they can make a quick return on a litter of pups or by puppy farmers. There are top quality chocolate pups available from a number of show-breeders who breed them responsibly and from proven bloodlines and there are now a handful of breeders of very capable working Labradors who are concentrating on this colour. Chocolate Labradors bred for the pet market are not recommended as working dogs but the careful combination of genetics from working dogs – chocolate and black – that will produce chocolate pups with working ability, is now underway. Any poor reputation that chocolate Labradors may have as working gundogs has nothing to do with their colour but everything to do with the way they are bred.

Fenway Brock – even working Labradors should retain the typical
head and expression that is the hallmark of the breed

David and Carol
Coode's Ch Warringahs
Gundaroo JW – a very
successful show winner
demonstrating his
natural working ability
*(Photo: Sharon Rogers)*

There appears to be no move on the part of the Kennel Club to address the fact that the vast majority of Labradors it registers every year are produced from working bloodlines and yet many don't look anything like its breed standard. It's a situation that makes it all the more important for prospective buyers of working Labradors to become fully conversant with the type of Labrador they may end up owning because the breed isn't of 'standard issue'. And as we have discussed in this chapter, the divergence within the breed is far greater than simply a split between working and show types.

First-time owners of working Labradors often find themselves with a type of dog they didn't anticipate having to deal with – either in the way it looks or the way it behaves. In so many cases a well-reared litter of working Labrador pups appears to be no different to any other, but it's essential to find out as much as you can about the breeding and appearance of what lies behind the current generation to help you buy a pup that will grow into the type of dog you expect it to – not only in looks but in ability, temperament and good health.

# CHAPTER TWO

·

# Buying the Right Labrador

·

**F**OR A BREED AS POPULAR as the Labrador it's easy to assume that finding a pup, a part-trained youngster or even a fully-trained adult dog would present few problems. Any initial internet search will reveal a huge number of Labrador litters on the market and while some may be described as being bred from dogs with working pedigrees, there is far more involved in making sure you acquire the right pup to suit your needs other than simply buying from a working-bred litter.

A working-bred pup will be from parents of appropriate breeding, but before any selection is made there are several other important criteria that must be taken into consideration: The 'breeding' behind the pup – in other words its pedigree – is paramount. Understanding and being able to 'read' – or perhaps decipher is a better word to use – a pedigree is an extremely useful tool for a puppy buyer and certainly an enlightening one. In fact it's equally relevant whether you are buying a pup, youngster or adult. It's also essential to know the health status of a pup's parents and that means seeing certificates for their hip scores, elbow scores and eye test results. Although several DNA tests concerning Labrador health issues are also now being undertaken by the most responsible breeders, I believe the OptiGen DNA test covering *prcd*PRA (blindness) and the DNA test for CNM (centro nuclear myopathy) of the parents are the most important and must be made

A young, part-trained dog – bright-eyed and ready for action!

available for inspection by the breeder. The temperament of the parents must also be taken into account. You will be able to assess the bitch when you inspect the litter but a first-hand appraisal of the sire may be unlikely – he could well come from the other end of the country! In that case it pays to do a bit of detective work and in particular to check-out what type of pups he's producing – possibly strong and confident or sensitive and less-outgoing. Best to know this information before taking the plunge. And finally make sure the parents are both good examples and typical of the breed and that the pup has been responsibly reared.

The aim should be to buy a pup or youngster with the breeding and temperament that suits you and provides you with a dog you can satisfactorily train to fulfil the working role you have planned. Quite often a pup or a youngster is bought to train as a working gundog but turns out to be totally unsuitable for the novice. So time and effort devoted to looking for the right pup or dog is never wasted. We hear people refer to their youngster as being 'too hot' when facing training challenges they hadn't anticipated.

In these cases the dog is usually very talented but has training require-ments beyond the capabilities of the novice handler – and there can also be additional behavioural issues. All can be avoided by making a considered decision at the outset.

A myriad of reasons are given by novices who encounter problems with their first dog. In many cases there has been a basic lack of understanding of what's required in terms of management and handling from a very early age, but more often than not it's simply a result of buying a pup without thoroughly assessing the type of dog you want to end up with and how to ensure you achieve that.

Finding the right pup or youngster shouldn't be an onerous task. It should be a pleasant and enjoyable experience – a journey that will yield valuable information and knowledge along the way about the dog your are hopefully about to spend the next 12 years or so of your life with.

So how do you avoid the pitfalls? Let's start off with buying a pup. All pups are difficult to resist but it's advisable not to start looking at litters without first having done some homework. All too often the heart can rule the head and even though you may go to look at a litter with the inten-tion of no more than just taking a look, despite all your best efforts the inevitable may happen. Unplanned and impulsive puppy purchase should be avoided at all costs!

Friends and others from local shoots may well have a litter of pups at precisely the time you're ready to make a commitment. Again, the tempta-tion can be all too great so while these litters may offer a convenient oppor-tunity it's important to subject such litters to the same intense scrutiny you should give to any other litter owned by a complete stranger. Don't feel duty bound to buy from a friend or acquaintance if the litter in question doesn't meet all your criteria. Always remember that to rear a pup, and to train and manage a young Labrador, you are going to invest a considerable amount of time and energy not to mention cost.

The pup's pedigree, the health status of its parents – which will be relevant to the pup's health in later life – its temperament and the way it has been reared are the most important items on your checklist. Addressing these basic issues from the start will avoid problems later.

And don't allow a lower price to tempt you to cut corners on what you're really looking for. A pup bought from a friend or acquaintance – or the last of a litter being sold at a reduced price – may seem like a bargain

An eight-week-old working-bred pup – good looks need not be the sole preserve of the show-ring

too good to miss but saving a few pounds on the initial cost when there's a risk of ending up with a raft of issues you hadn't bargained for is false economy.

Never lose sight of what it is you actually require from an adult working Labrador. So continually remind yourself of what you're really looking for. If you need a Labrador to be a one-day-a-week peg dog during the shooting season and live as part of the family for the rest of the time your needs will be very different from the person with a greater year-round commitment to shooting or to someone whose aspirations are driven by success at working tests or field trials.

While all of this may appear to be taking the job of buying a pup to the extreme, I can assure you that any time spent is worth it. Finding out as much as you can about a litter and its background before taking the plunge and making a purchase, will be of immeasurable value compared with the realisation some months down the line when you have a young dog on your hands that is either proving difficult to train, is clearly unsuitable for the job you intended or worse still has shown early signs of health problems.

So where do you start the search for a new pup? Litters of pups sired by field trial champions are considered to be a safe bet, especially by those buying a Labrador pup for the first time. In these cases the sire of the litter has demonstrated his ability as a competitive working dog and has won his title and that will clearly come through in his pups. But that in itself doesn't mean all his progeny will inherit his ability. All sires only pass on a proportion of their genes – good and bad – and some are better at passing on good genes than others. In all livestock breeding top winners can't be guaranteed to replicate their superiority when the females they are mated to may have obvious faults that can predominate in the progeny.

And some sires – be they dogs, horses or whatever – are better 'producers' than others. The world of working Labradors is no exception. There will always be well known field trial champions that leave a definite 'stamp' on their progeny and earn a reputation for being prepotent sires. Others may be less so. Always remember that the inherited working qualities of any progeny are taking 50% of their genes from the dam. So before getting too carried away by an opportunity to buy a pup sired by a particularly fashionable field trial champion it's essential to find out more about his progeny and how generous he is at passing on his superior genes – and that's before you even start to consider anything about the dam of the litter. More of her later.

All field trial champions have been extremely well trained in order to achieve a very high standard of work that was good enough for them to achieve their titles. But the level of excellence they have attained also has a lot to do with the expertise of the trainer – and some dogs will undoubtedly have demanded more skilled training to achieve the end result than others. Clearly a novice trainer cannot expect to have that level of experience and yet the progeny of that dog may well take after the sire and require it. So my advice is to find out as much about the sire as possible and about the reputation of his progeny in terms of their trainability.

For a novice buying a pup for the first time and having the choice of buying from a litter sired by either a field trial champion dog that may not be the most exciting in his work but is a solid and reliable worker, compared with another sire with a reputation for being fast and with lots of 'pazzaz', which would you choose? The second dog is obviously a dog with ability and drive but qualities that need an experienced trainer to fully exploit and control. Pups sired by the first dog are more likely to suit a novice provided

Field trials can provide an important insight into the world of working Labradors for those about to buy a pup or a youngster
(*Photo: Peter Bates*)

OPPOSITE PAGE
An eight-month-old working-bred pup – good head, good bone and ready for school!

enough can be found out about the type of pups he has produced. There will always be outstanding field trial champions siring biddable, trainable pups but there will also be those whose titles have been won more by the influence of expert trainers who have been able to harness the challenges presented by brilliance.

It isn't difficult to find out about the trainability of the progeny of the leading field trial champions of the day and to make a judgement as to how those dogs are 'breeding' – especially if they are popular sires. But let's turn now to the bitch and her role in influencing the working ability of her progeny.

Try and find out as much as you can about her in terms of her breeding, health status, working ability and temperament and wherever possible the ability and traits of any pups she may have produced in a previous litter.

Many owners of working Labrador bitches decide to breed a litter of pups. As in all things there are good bitches and there are not so good bitches, but all too often the owner elects to use a field trial champion as the sire – a choice primarily made on the basis of assuming the litter will be easier to sell and also that the pups will inherit the superior working ability

of the sire. That may well be the case just as the dogs that win the annual International Gundog League (IGL) Retriever Championship, the highest accolade in field trials, always attract plenty of bitches whose owners hope that similar greatness will be bestowed upon the forthcoming litter and that selling them will present no problem.

If you don't know the owner of a litter you are considering buying a pup from you will most probably have to take his or her word for it when it comes to an assessment of the bitch's qualities as a worker. You are unlikely to be told of any of her shortcomings – she may be 'hot' and hard to handle, she may be gun-shy, she may have a 'squeak' or she may be hard-mouthed. These are faults you certainly don't want and yet they are faults that may well manifest themselves in her progeny no matter how good the sire. So the more you can find out about the bitch the better placed you will be in your decision making.

If the bitch has had a previous litter there is no harm in asking the owner if you could contact someone who already has one of her progeny. That may at least give you an insight into what she produces. The 'not so good' working Labrador bitches will not be prevented from passing on their shortcomings simply because the sire was an accomplished field trial champion, so while there are many title holders producing top quality pups, a litter's potential must never be solely assessed on the sire's achievements.

Of course there are a great many litters sired by dogs that have never been near a field trial. There are very good working dogs whose owners simply don't feel the need to compete as a means of having their dog's working ability confirmed, but there are also other less good dogs that are used to sire litters for all sorts of reasons. It may be that these dogs just happened to be local to the bitch, possibly owned by a friend or it may be that the mating was a free one to 'prove' the dog as a sire. If you are looking at a litter sired by a dog that is totally unknown to you it's advisable to find out as much about the dog as you can in terms of his ability, pedigree and temperament – and to make sure he at least has had his hips and elbows X-rayed and his eyes tested.

This effort will be rewarded when you find a litter that meets your needs because buying a pup that isn't suitable is the easy option and probably why many novice owners find it difficult to train their first dog. It's often the owner's lack of experience as a trainer that gets the blame whereas it's far more likely to be that the wrong pup was bought in the first place.

If the lure of competition is the main attraction of owning a working Labrador, it's important to know how to distinguish between a litter of working-bred pups that will fulfil their purpose in life as purely shooting or picking-up dogs, and a litter of pups with the breeding that should produce rather more in terms of ability, drive, style and inherent 'game sense' that's so essential for competing at field trials.

Resisting the temptation to rush headlong into making a purchase will pay handsome dividends in the long term. Let caution be your guide but equally enjoy the time spent researching the breed, talking to breeders and looking at as many 'types' of Labradors at work as you can. The pay-off will hopefully mean you won't become the owner of a nine-month-old hooligan that's running rings around you or end-up making desperate phone calls to the nearest gundog trainer in the hope of bailing you out of a hurried purchase.

If you are totally new to the breed and have never owned a working Labrador I suggest it's worth taking some time to look at a wide range of Labradors 'in action' – at field trials, at working tests and in the shooting

A nine-month-old working-bred pup – even pups from field trial breeding should have good conformation

field. The Kennel Club can provide all the information you need regarding contact details for field trial societies and gundog clubs that organise tests and trials. It will also provide details of all the regional Labrador clubs – as well as The Labrador Retriever Club which is the 'parent' club of the breed – which stage working tests during the spring and summer and field trials during the autumn and winter. The secretaries of these clubs are always keen to help and advise and provided you make it known that you want to attend a trial as a spectator you certainly will find it a very useful experience in helping you build up an impression of Labradors working at a high standard of competition.

Working tests held in the spring and summer attract Labradors from a wide spectrum – including dogs that have also competed in field trials, others that restrict their competitive outings purely to the test season and possibly even show-bred dogs that have an aptitude for work. All the regional breed clubs hold working tests so again it's a case of making the contact and attending the event to watch, listen and learn.

Be acutely aware of what you want in your working dog – in the job you ultimately have in mind for it and in the confidence you have in yourself to train the dog. Consider too the temperament of a dog you feel would best suit you and your family and even how you want the dog to look. Close observation at both field trials and working tests can provide an enormous amount of first-hand knowledge that cannot be gleaned from a book or on-screen. So watch the dogs and the handlers and you should start to see what 'type' of dog you feel would be most suitable for you. Note the way different dogs work, the way they respond to be handled and even how they look. It's all grist to the mill that will greatly assist you as you identify breeders to contact or litters of pups you may be interested in.

Of course field trials are restricted to the number of dogs competing – less so with working tests – but nevertheless you may feel you have only scratched the surface and not seen enough Labradors actually working. To help you gain as much information as possible from the dogs you have seen working it's worthwhile listing those that appealed and making a note of their breeding – their sire and dam. This will give you important information for the next stage.

If the dogs were bred by those who were handling them on the day you could make a direct contact. If they were not you need to identify the breeders of any dogs noted and do likewise. This may seem a time consuming process but instead of leaping into the unknown and buying on a whim or just because a litter was close by or even sired by a well known field trial champion, it's enabling you to have an insight into the finished article.

If observing at first-hand isn't an option a similar process should be undertaken but one that circumvents the actual attendance at trials or tests but equally avoids any impulse buying.

Through the shooting press and via the internet it's not difficult to locate well known breeders of working Labradors. Some will breed primarily to produce Labradors of field-trial standard but there will always be pups and youngsters from these breeders ready to be sold to those looking for a quality dog for shooting or for picking-up. There are other established breeders who don't compete with their dogs but have an excellent reputation for producing top class working Labradors.

If you can glean any recommendations from others or are impressed enough by what you see on a web-site or in an advert, contact should be made to discuss the availability of dogs for sale. Arrange a visit to the breeder and look at the dogs. Take note of how the dogs react to their

Two bitches from the Fabracken kennel — part of the kennel's hard-working picking-up team (*Photo: Anne Taylor*)

handler and as well as any impressive demonstrations you will inevitably be given, be mindful of the dogs' attitude and temperament. It's important to stress here that once you feel you have located someone that you trust and feel can provide you with a Labrador that will fulfil your needs, it may well be necessary to order a pup from a future litter if none are currently available. A few months wait at the start will be well worth while if it ensures you can become the owner of the right dog.

## Where to buy

Because of the popularity of the Labrador there are always plenty of litters on the market. Many are from one-litter owners others are from responsible breeders who pursue their interest in the breed as a hobby or even a business if it's run alongside training or allied canine interests. Lastly there are those produced by puppy farmers – many of whom may not actually appear to be so. The latter fall into two categories. There are those who operate at low standards in all that they do and there are others who present a respectable picture to their potential customers but are basically running a business to produce as many pups as they can by keeping a large number of bitches managed on a commercial breeding scale. These 'volume' breeders, provided the sire and dam of all their pups are Kennel Club registered, have the right to register the pups in the same way as responsible breeders. So it's important to remember that a Kennel Club registered pup is in no way a 'seal of approval' in terms of the pup's quality or how it has been reared.

The Kennel Club's Approved Breeders Scheme has been created to try to help puppy buyers locate pups bred by 'approved' breeders.

While there are always many one-off litters on the market, it pays to make enquiries fully-armed with all the relevant questions as discussed in this chapter. Well-meaning breeders of an individual litter may be genuinely ignorant of all manner of issues that are important to you as a prospective owner. So ensure all is as it should be before you inspect the litter.

Recommendation is hard to beat when it comes to buying anything and if you know someone who has bought a pup and is highly satisfied with it as an adult then you could do a lot worse than take the same route if that's the type of Labrador you are looking for as a working dog. Of course all the well known kennels will breed litters from time to time and if you are convinced you want a pup from a particular bloodline it's worth waiting for. Your name will have to go on to a waiting list but hopefully the wait will be well worth while.

As mentioned previously in this chapter the regional Labrador clubs and the Labrador Retriever Club itself are an excellent starting point in the search for a pup. Local gundog clubs, the shooting press and the range of gundog web-sites as well as those of individual breeders will all provide useful information.

## Cost

The price you can expect to pay for a pup, a part-trained or even a fully-trained Labrador varies greatly but as in most cases you tend to get what you pay for. Yes, there are Labrador pups available at rock-bottom prices of around £400 or even less if the owner of a litter is desperate to sell. Well-bred pups from responsible breeders range from £650 to £850 but even if

The natural ability to retrieve is hard to resist even at this age (*Photo: Sharon Rogers*)

you have to pay more than that it is still a very small investment for something that will hopefully give you at least a decade of work as your shooting dog. Similarly part-trained dogs can range hugely in price. Some that appear on the market for little more than puppy price are usually trying to be sold quickly – quite often because they have developed a fault in their training or because some other unwanted trait has developed.

Part-trained dogs should be at least double the cost of a pup so a breeder with a good reputation for his stock and who charges £850 for pups would expect to sell anything part-trained for £1600 upwards. That's only a very general guide – some will be more and some less but beware anything that looks too cheap. Fully-trained Labradors are the top of the heap but again can vary enormously in price. Expect to pay at least £3000 and probably more if a dog has some competitive ability.

## Health checks

### Hips

Hips are X-rayed once in a dog's life when the dog is over 12-months old. From a year-old the hips are considered to have fully developed. They are X-rayed by a vet who then submits the X-ray plates for 'scoring'. This is undertaken by another vet who is a member of the 'panel' of the British Veterinary Association/Kennel Club scheme and is authorised to award a score for both hips. In simple terms the score is based on the way the 'ball and socket' joint of the hip fits together. Any abnormality that may cause the hip joint not to work properly and subsequently increase the risk of hip-dysplasia will be identified by the vet. A perfect score for both hips is 0.0 but the total joint score for both hips should be under 15 – which is the current breed average.

Hip dysplasia is a hereditary problem and so far the X-ray system has been the only way of making sure Labradors with low hip scores are bred from. But it is only a 'snapshot' of that dog who may well have untested littermates with high hip scores. To give breeders a much more effective strategy to eliminate hip problems in Labradors a DNA test is being developed.

It's still in the early stages of development but will be a valuable tool to breeders when it becomes available. Because it's hereditary and genetic inheritance can be full of surprises, there is always a risk that two dogs mated together – both with acceptable hip scores – can produce some progeny with high scores. There is another school of thought that believes good hips can be adversely affected when youngsters are allowed excessive exercise. It is recommended as a basic part of sensible and responsible management of pups and youngsters that they are not allowed too much free running, jumping or any other activity that may have a bad effect on any part of their physical development – and hips are a part of that. Similarly under-exercise can have an equally deleterious effect by restricting natural development, so it's important to monitor exercise in young and growing Labradors, not to allow excessive free-running but equally not to over-restrict activity.

## Elbows

Although the need to have hips X-rayed is widely acknowledged, the importance of assessing the development of the elbow joints is less so and yet it is equally important. Often referred to as 'puppy lameness' it is still not uncommon to find the condition of osteo-chondritis (OCD) termed as such by those who are unaware of the problems that can beset the elbows. Although the causes for the onset of OCD are not fully understood, it is now increasingly important to have elbows X-rayed at the same time as hips (again elbows can be assessed any time from 12-months of age). While there is clearly a hereditary influence, the impact of environment, diet and exercise is thought to play a part. OCD is most commonly identified in pups from four-months old. Often it occurs in heavily boned and well-grown pups but that is by no means a precursor to being prone. OCD is caused by a malformation of the bone surfaces within the elbow joint. Small particles of bone can become loose and affect the cartilage resulting in lameness. The level of lameness can vary from an occasional limp to more severe symptoms. A high protein diet fed for too long or allowing a strong well grown pup to place undue pressure on the elbow joints by excessive 'pounding' from too much galloping exercise or even being allowed to jump too early, can all be contributory factors. A perfect elbow score is 0.0 and the scores rise to 3 on each side. Questions should be asked about breeding from any dog that shows even a 0.1 elbow score although some bitches with this level of problem are bred from if care is taken to mate them to a dog that

A seven-week-old Fenway pup – good looking with plenty of bone and a good head. This puppy already has a true, Labrador double-coat

has a 0.0 score. However my advice would be not to breed from any bitch showing any risk of perpetuating the problem. Responsible rearing, taking note of diet and exercise is also important.

## Eye checks

The Labrador Retriever can suffer from several eye diseases of which Hereditary Cataract (HC) and Generalised Progressive Retinal Atrophy (GPRA) are the two most common.

The OptiGen *prcd*PRA Test is DNA-based that identifies one form of Progressive Retinal Atrophy (PRA) and so helps breeders avoid matings where genetics can lead to affected progeny.

PRA refers to a group of diseases that result in degeneration of the retina over a period of time leading to declining vision and eventual blindness. The letters 'prcd' stand for 'progressive rod-cone degeneration' which is the type of PRA found in Labradors. All dogs and bitches used for breeding should have an annual eye test undertaken by a veterinary ophthalmologist under the BVA/KC Eye Scheme. This is in addition to any DNA testing that breeders may wish to carry out.

## Exercise Induced Collapse – EIC

The Exercise Induced Collapse syndrome does occur is some Labradors. The DNA test for EIC hasn't been widely taken up by breeders although the condition – which causes sufferers to collapse during strenuous exercise – has been recognised in some working dogs for many years. While it's always important to know the full health status of the parents of any puppy – and EIC tests can be part of that – I don't believe the absence of EIC testing results should be regarded as a barrier to buying a pup. Dogs affected with EIC initially start to wobble on their legs during exercise and then collapse – a state in which they can remain for several minutes. Although most recover, the disease can sometimes be fatal.

## Centronuclear Myopathy – CNM

Pups suffering from CNM show a degree of weight-loss from about two weeks old. By about four weeks affected pups fail to demonstrate any reflexes in the tendon and as they develop and start to walk it's clear they have difficulty moving normally – a condition caused by a weakening of the muscles. There is now a DNA test for CNM.

## Health check list

Hips – X-ray from 12-months old

Elbows – X-ray from 12-months old

Eyes – ophthalmic test annually from 12-months old

Eyes – DNA test (Optigen)

Centronuclear Myopathy – DNA test

Exercise Induced Collapse – DNA test

## Why the main health tests are important

The purchase of any pup or youngster must take account of the health status of both parents. Responsible breeders are taking every possible step to produce healthy Labradors. Others who breed litters of pups from non-health checked parents are selling pups that are at much greater risk of succumbing to one of the health issues that can occur in the breed. Unfortunately there are still large numbers of individuals producing litters of working Labradors who pay little or no heed to the full and necessary remit of health testing. It's irresponsible and no one about to buy a Labrador pup and prepared to invest in its rearing and future training should take the risk of owning anything other than a pup whose parents have both been fully health checked. To ignore the importance of these health checks is unwise and can prove extremely costly.

While responsible breeders take every care to ensure any pups they produce are as healthy as possible, the unpredictability of genetics can sometimes produce the unexpected. Even Labradors from fully health tested parents can develop hip or elbow problems or shows signs of other hereditary problems that may be lurking in their genealogical make-up.

The Labrador as a breed would be in a much poorer state of health and there would be far more dogs suffering from physical debilitations if breeders hadn't embraced the level of testing undertaken over the last 30 years.

Untested bitches that are genetic 'carriers' of the genes for *prcd*PRA or CNM will still produce a proportion of their progeny that are also carriers for these hereditary health problems even when mated to a sire tested as 'clear'. So a pup from this type of alliance that turns out to be a carrier for possibly *prcd*PRA or CNM will produce pups that are 'affected' – in other words will suffer from premature blindness or will contract CNM – if mated to a dog that is also a carrier because a carrier mated to a carrier produces affected pups. Far easier to eliminate all this uncertainty at the outset and buy a pup from a litter produced by two fully health tested parents.

It is pertinent to consider the views held by some breeders that the Labrador could be heading towards a situation of 'over-testing' in pursuit of healthy Labradors. These views emanate from a belief that it is never going to be possible to eliminate all healthy issues and that the risk is a gradual narrowing of the gene pool while in pursuance of health above all else. In my opinion X-ray scoring for hips and elbows, annual eye testing and DNA testing for *prcd*PRA and CNM is a fairly comprehensive package and one that should form the basis for all breeders. If a new Labrador owner buys a pup or youngster from stock with that level of health testing they are doing all they can to acquire a healthy pup.

Walking-up at a working test – a good opportunity to see dogs at work *(Photo: Sharon Rogers)*

## Reading a pedigree

A pedigree is a document that shows the genealogy of a dog – its parentage. A pup's pedigree usually shows four or five generations of the breeding 'behind' the pup – in other words its ancestry. It must be pointed out that the majority of individuals breeding litters of Labrador pups will produce a genuine and correct pedigree certificate to anyone enquiring about the litter or anyone who buys a pup. But there is no actual 'policing' of pedigrees and I have seen pedigrees that I have known to include errors – genuine or maybe not. Because there is nothing to stop anyone 'concocting' a pedigree to make it more attractive in terms of the number of successful field trial winners that appear in the ancestry it may be worth while having an experienced eye cast over the pedigree of a pup you are considering.

For many people who buy a Labrador pup for work the pedigree is little more than a piece of paper with names on it. But with a little knowledge – and perhaps the help of someone with experience of breeding – a pedigree can provide an enormous amount of information. So while many puppy buyers don't even see a pedigree until the day they actually buy the pup, in my opinion the pedigree should be the very first thing that's looked at – I would even go so far as to say it should be looked at before the litter itself.

While some pedigrees now contain additional information relating to health check results, at this stage let's concentrate on the primary role of a pedigree as a register of ancestry. The name of the male will be directly above the female as each mating creates the pedigree's format. This makes it easy to trace the lineage. The pedigrees of well-bred Labradors will contain names of individual dogs and bitches that are 'prefixed' by a kennel name. That 'prefix' or 'affix' as it is now referred to by the Kennel Club, is owned solely by one breeder and is his or her trademark. All dogs bred in that particular kennel carry that name. So it may be that the same kennel 'affixes' crop up several times in one pedigree as they appear in front of the names of various ancestors. For example Fenway Brock – 'Fenway' is my affix.

All these dogs/bitches are registered with the Kennel Club but the Kennel Club will also register dogs without an affix so there may well be dogs/bitches appearing in the pedigree with names like 'Swift Sally' or 'Black Bob'. These may well be registered but a proliferation of dogs/bitches in a pedigree that do not carry an affix can suggest a weakness in the depth of good breeding within that pedigree.

The Kennel Club has now introduced a system via its web-site that enables a check to be made concerning the amount of in-breeding of a particular dog. While this is a tool the Kennel Club is now encouraging puppy buyers to use it is important not to confuse in-breeding with line-breeding. While no one wants to buy a pup that is closely 'in-bred', a pup whose pedigree can be seen to show skilful line-breeding – in other words where similar bloodlines have been carefully used to maintain the qualities of a certain strain or type – should pose no weakness as a result.

If you have taken some time to find out information about the sire and the dam of the litter and their immediate ancestors you should have an insight into the pups' likely ability and, hopefully, trainability. All the well-used stud dogs have traits they are known for. Try and find out as much as you can about the predominant sires in the pedigree to help give you some idea of what that bloodline is likely to produce.

There is a range of terminology that needs to be learnt. The initials FT Ch in front of a dog or bitch's name means Field Trial Champion. Sh Ch means Show Champion and Ch means Champion (referring to a show dog that has won his title in the ring and also passed a basic test of his working ability by achieving success in the KC's working gundog certificate). Some pedigrees may also indicate working test wins with the initials WTA which refers to working test award or WTW which means working test winner.

## Buying a part-trained Labrador

Part-trained is a term that even I find almost impossible to precisely define because so much depends on the dog itself as well as its age – both of which determine how far it has progressed in training. The desire for a 'part-trained' Labrador usually comes from those who really just don't want the hassle of puppyhood and all its trials and tribulations and prefer to take-on something that's ready to make the transition into serious training.

To make a culinary analogy, if a young, part-trained Labrador was a potato you'd call it 'par-boiled' but like potatoes, if you cook them too quickly even the best start to fall apart.

And that's one of the main issues buyers face when trying to find a part-trained dog that fits the criteria they have in mind. Most of the time those who believe that buying a part-trained youngster is the preferred route to gundog ownership often expect far too much of these raw teenagers.

We all know that the big fear in most peoples' minds is the reason why a young dog is being sold in the first place. Is it simply because the seller has seen something he doesn't like or noticed a trait he knows will only get worse as the dog matures. Yes, the higher priced part-trained dogs are clearly those who, for their age, are doing more in terms of training, but I've seen more than a few part-trained dogs that have obviously been pushed-on too far too quickly in their training and yet to the novice buyer appear to be a tremendous prospect.

For some unscrupulous dealers the best way to 'move on' a young dog with a fault is to go full-tilt at its training so that it appears to be very accomplished when in fact what the potential buyer sees is rather a sham. The training of the dog has been rushed and it has possibly received some very firm handling to achieve a quick, albeit fragile, education.

Once home with the new owner, and under a far less stringent training regime, the cracks can soon start to appear. What seemed to be a very well advanced youngster under 12-months old and one only needing a bit of polish around the edges, may begin to crumble just like those over-cooked spuds!

As we have said, buying the so-called 'part-trained' Labrador appeals to those who haven't the time, facilities or the interest in rearing a pup and to those who genuinely feel they need to take-on something that is past the 'silly' stage and is starting to learn what its future life entails. But then there are others who come at this option purely from the costs involved.

Buying a part-trained Labrador from a well established and reputable source should not be a viewed as a low-cost exercise. I am not going to quote prices at the top end of the scale here, but I will venture to say that anyone with a good reputation who offers a part-trained dog for sale will be asking a fair price – but not a low price.

But that's not to say that there are 'so-called' part-trained Labradors on the market for little more than the price of a good pup. These need to be treated with great caution. Buying something that has been 'started' should not be undertaken purely as a means of getting better value than buying a pup.

So what can you expect from a part-trained dog? The answer to that depends on its age and on the dog, and I suggest that anyone looking for a part-trained Labrador beefs up on what these youngsters are expected to be doing at certain stages. If you are offered an 'all singing and dancing' 12-month-old dog that looks as though it has been 'over cooked', tread with the greatest care.

If you are offered a 10-month-old genuine, happy youngster that's clearly listening to its owner, is responsive, respectful but probably still sloppy in its heelwork and with a clear but not polished ability to retrieve, that's probably going to make the better dog. It may be a bit over-enthusiastic and it may be raw, but ask yourself is it happy in its job and look into its eyes. That will tell you a lot. The 'empty-eyed' youngster that has been sent to boot camp far too soon is the tell tale sign.

Of course it's essential to make sure the dog is in good physical condition and that you see all the Kennel Club paperwork regarding registrations. Hip, elbow and eye certificates are essential if it's over 12-months old and of course vaccination certificates.

Some of the tales I hear about part-trained dogs being offered for sale are worrying – not only for the dogs involved but for the unsuspecting people who have been to see them as potential purchasers. I once sold a puppy to a young man who had been to see a part-trained dog advertised on the inter-

A well-reared working-bred pup with a lovely, kind head and expression

net at what he described as 'a big kennels'. The dog was described to me as being 'half starved' and seemingly so nervous it wouldn't go near him but was then put through its paces in a paddock spending the last few yards of each retrieve almost on its belly. Fortunately he resisted making the purchase although he was tempted out of concern for the dog's welfare.

I sold another dog to a man who had actually bought a dog that growled at him when he went to see it! It too produced an adequate demonstration of its skills and as the buyer was going to kennel the dog outside rather than in the house he decided to take a chance. The last thing I heard was that the dog had run off the first time it had been taken out for training and hadn't been seen since!

For those who buy part-trained dogs ready to work in the coming season it's wise not to expect too much too soon. Whatever training has been undertaken at home or out shooting a few rabbits will not fully prepare the dog for a driven day or for a full day's picking-up if he's too young. So take it steady. There will be temptations galore that will bring new pressures to your relationship – ones that may not yet have been fully tested.

Don't rush young dogs that have been bought part-trained and hopefully finished; don't have a dog out for every drive on his first day's shooting with you; far better to give him less work and for him to stay focussed on you rather than launching him into a full-blown day and weakening those bonds of control and understanding that you have hopefully achieved.

There are those who own a dog to shoot, rather than shoot to own a dog, and in the former case I so often see Labradors looking rather forlorn and lacking any verve, trailing along at the side of the owner. Invariably these dogs have been bought as 'part-trained' adornments to the kit and do their job very clinically, but I have to say don't always look too happy about life.

So if you are considering buying a part-trained youngster my advice is to buy something that has not had its spirit crushed just so that it can demonstrate a 100 yard retrieve at 12-months old and flatten to the stop whistle as though it was going to be run over by a train. Go for the dog that is happy, has manners, is attentive and has raw ability. And before you sally forth into the shooting field make sure you use the early days to re-affirm your relationship amidst the new and exciting challenges you will both encounter.

# CHAPTER THREE

·

# Modern Life –
# the 21st Century Labrador

D OG OWNERSHIP IN the 21st century is considered by some to be too demanding when expected to fit into a busy lifestyle. Inevitably that perception deters any thought of embarking upon such a commitment – and particularly taking on the responsibility of a working gundog. With spare time seeming to be in ever shortening supply and the fact that many homes aren't occupied for part of the day, many would-be owners of working Labradors are naturally cautious.

While it's essential to be able to met the daily needs of a working Labrador – be that as a house dog or a dog kennelled outside – the amount of time that can be spent with a pup or a youngster is also extremely important. But that doesn't necessarily mean modern family life can't accommodate a Labrador that can ultimately fulfil its role as working gundog.

It has to be said that dog ownership isn't advisable for those who are away from their home all day, every day. But where there's a degree of flexibility – perhaps someone is at home on certain days of the week or where a member of the family works part-time – various options can be con-sidered to help ownership of a working Labrador become a reality – and a very satisfying one at that!

However compromises have to be sought to avoid leaving dogs in isolation for long periods. Working gundogs are no different to any other

Spending plenty of time
with young pups from
an early age lays the
foundation of a life-long
partnership

dog despite the fact that their role in life seems to wrongly imply to some owners that they are more enduring of hardship. While it's a sad fact that many working Labradors spend too much time alone – a situation that inevitably leads to training and often behavioural issues – I hope this chapter will provide useful guidelines to improve the way that 'home alone' Labradors can be more successfully managed.

Ideally someone who is in a position to either have a dog with them all the time or has a family-life situation where there is always someone at home, is always the preferred basis for successful dog ownership. But in reality many pups and young dogs are brought into life-style situations that aren't ideal but are ones to which the dog must adapt. So it's far better to be fully aware of what's actually required at the outset in order to ensure the dog's welfare isn't jeopardised.

The key is being able to plan and to instigate a way of management and care that meets the dog's needs and which fit in with the owner's life-style while still producing a well-balanced and happy gundog.

Before we look at how this can best be achieved let's first consider the raw material – the working Labrador. This is a highly intelligent breed whose intuition and ability to learn will be at the heart of your relationship and the progress you achieve in training.

Many of the issues encountered by first-time owners when starting to train working Labradors are partly caused by shortcomings in the daily management of their dogs and the routine – or lack of it – they employ. Yes, as a breed working Labradors are extremely tolerant and adaptable – probably more than most gundog breeds – but it's unfair to expect a dog or a young pup to endure long periods devoid of human contact and then to suddenly respond and go into learning mode 'at the flick of a switch' when the owner comes home. This isn't the ideal way to produce a dog that's in the right frame of mind and receptive to training.

Routine is the bedrock of successful dog management, whether managing one dog or 20 dogs. Providing a routine can be quickly established to deliver the proper care and attention a good foundation will be laid for the future.

The early and most formative stages of a dog's life are extremely important to its mental and physical development. Unfortunately when corners are cut in terms of day to day management – albeit unintentionally – behavioural issues and even training problems can occur.

Fenway Timber –
a good looking
chocolate Labrador
bred from working
lines

## Kennel life

Kennelling a dog in a home situation has become an increasingly popular option providing flexibility for the owner and – providing it's of a high standard – a relaxed and natural environment for a working gundog. Certainly for those who don't want to have a dog in the house the decision to invest in a kennel and run outside can be an ideal compromise. Some dogs that are kennelled aren't allowed in the house at all while others lead a dual life-style and are allowed inside at certain times.

There is now a vast array of kennels and runs on the market to suit all needs and budgets and made from a range of materials and a multitude of designs. I would firmly advise the purchase of the best kennel you can afford – cutting corners on cost can be counterproductive. This structure is hopefully going to last the dog its entire lifetime so this is a one-off purchase and it needs to be considered carefully.

I always recommend buying a kennel in which the owner can actually stand up – and to look very carefully at how secure the kennel is in terms

Weld-mesh panels can provide a flexible and durable kennel system

of preventing unwanted entry. Gundog theft is widespread and while we'll consider various security measures later in this chapter, it's initially important to consider the robustness of a kennel and what security measures can be applied to it.

Kennels are now available in fibreglass and heavy duty plastic, but timber kennels remain the most popular. However it's important when looking at timber kennels to consider the 'chew risk'. Most Labradors enjoy chewing wood and even if they grow out of the habit as adults, determined pups and youngsters can achieve a considerable amount of damage to all unprotected timber edges within the building. Manufacturers will fit anti-chew strips on request, something I would certainly recommend.

The 'run' section of a kennel – constructed of wire mesh although bars have become increasingly popular – may be an integral part of the construction or can be added on. Ideally the run area should be covered to provide protection from the worst of the weather as well as shade from intense sunshine and it's important to ensure that any rain-water run-off from the roof is guttered away and not allowed to fall into the kennel area.

The main section of the kennel will be the area that provides the dog with its sleeping quarters and somewhere offering additional shelter during the daytime. Ideally this section should also provide an area in which the dog can be kept securely during the night – this is safer for the dog and avoids the risk of night-time barking which is more likely to occur if the dog has free access to the run area day and night and becomes alarmed by something unexpected. The sleeping area does need careful consideration because some designs simply have a sleeping box with a pop-hole constructed at the back of the kennel which means the dog cannot satisfactorily be confined at night.

A sleeping area in which the dog can be confined must be properly ventilated but a window must always be considered as a risk from both outside and inside. It's not unknown for dogs to break windows so not only do they need to be well above the dog's height of access and be 'meshed' for added protection, but they also need to be small enough to avoid unwanted entry.

All kennel sleeping areas should be lined with hardboard at least, and preferably with a 'sandwich' layer of hardboard and insulation to achieve maximum heat retention in the winter.

Many kennels come as a complete 'kennel and run' package but if you require a larger run area it's worth considering buying the actual kennel – which would include the dog's sleeping accommodation – and then constructing the run by adding purpose kennel-mesh or kennel-bar sections to the front and of the size you require. These are an excellent investment and if good quality sections are purchased they will last many years. They provide design flexibility and the option to 'add-on' and increase the run area if required.

Locate any kennel structure in a situation that isn't going to subject the dog to severe winds or intense sunlight, although banishing a kennel to the darkest corner of the garden is equally not advisable. Kennelled dogs enjoy seeing what's going on around them. Make sure the location of the kennel avoids any surface water draining back into the run and underneath the building. Ideally the run area should be concreted but well-laid concrete flags can be equally effective; both will enable the area to be kept clean. Earth, gravel, grass or wood-chip are not appropriate surfaces for dog kennel run areas, not only because they can't be kept clean but because they don't create a secure ground cover to avoid escape by digging!

Laying power to the kennel has considerable advantages to the owner. Being able to provide extra lighting in the winter and even to using a timer-switch to light the kennels if the owner is coming back late on winter days, are clear advantages. It may be that you decide to heat the kennel in the winter or, if you have a bitch and decide to breed from her and use the

Even I get a day off – working Labradors deserve a comfortable bed in their kennels

kennel for whelping, power for lighting and a heat-lamp will be essential. If power is laid to the kennel it should be undertaken professionally. All wiring and switches must be positioned taking account of the full adult height that any dog housed in the kennel can reach.

Power also allows dogs to benefit from day-time radio. Our kennels have a radio switched on all day long. It provides additional background sound for the dogs and while it means adult dogs don't have to spend time alone in an arid atmosphere of silence, it also provides a constant source of noise, talk and music that has a beneficial effect on pups and youngsters.

Kennel bedding is an ever vexed question. Labradors do like to curl up when they are asleep and in my experience generously sized plastic dog beds are hard to beat and the most cost effective option. However the heavy-duty deep-cushioned dog beds are provided for some of our kennelled oldies; they are not cheap but they are the ultimate in comfort; they are easily cleaned and very durable. In our plastic beds we use fleece dog bedding which can be bought from a wide range of suppliers; it's warm, easily washed and hard wearing. Alternatively a deep bed of soft wood

Soft, shredded paper bedding provides warmth and comfort for working dogs that are kennelled

shavings is an option; for dogs that will not tolerate fleece bedding we use soft, shredded paper or chopped cardboard as used for horses. Straw should not be used. We have used oat straw in the past but even though some kennels do have success with this there is the ever present risk that it can trigger skin irritations which can be difficult to cure, especially in winter when the treatment can involve bathing in medicated shampoo!

## Puppy routine

So how do you establish a routine for a pup that you ultimately want to live outside? I wouldn't advise buying an eight-week old pup and immediately putting it outside into a kennel. Being taken from its littermates is stressful enough but to confine it outside immediately simply aggravates a situation that is already putting undue pressure on the pup. So bring the pup into the house for a few weeks at least; use a cage in the house for part of that time but allow the pup freedom to get to know you and to settle and to be allowed free access to the kennel if possible. Gradually introduce the pup to what will be its home by feeding it in the kennel and give it a bone or similar treat in there so that the association is a positive one. Over time the transition from inside to outside can be achieved; there may be some resistance – probably vocal – but this should be addressed without any harsh negative response from you as the owner. All chastisement will do is exacerbate the stress on the part of the pup.

Winter is not the best time to start kennel training so select a time of year that will help you do the job more easily. As the pup develops and heads towards the landmark 'six month stage' it's important not to assume that size and *joie de vivre* signify that it can be left for long periods in a kennel with no human contact. This is a very important stage in the pup's development and the routine established should ensure the pup is getting an adequate amount of time with you or a member of the family as often as possible. To expect these youngsters to be closeted away for many hours and then come out of the kennel and stand to attention ready for training is expecting too much.

Many working Labradors have to learn to adapt to today's modern life style where their owners may well be away from the house for certain periods of the day. Unfortunately for the dogs there are some owners who leave adult dogs alone for the entire day and do so in the belief that they are none the worse for it. They are misguided in their assumption. It's a far from ideal system of management and not one that I condone. Yes, the dog will still be alive when you get back but vets are increasingly making it clear to owners who leave dogs for long periods that they are increasing the risk of health problems based on the refusal of many kennel dogs to be unclean in their kennel quarters. If we were prevented from access to a toilet every day for eight hours our health would soon suffer – and it's no different for dogs. However adult dogs will adapt to being left for certain periods provided they are not too long. Four hours is a length of time I consider long enough to leave an adult Labrador unattended. I know there are those who would think this underestimates the 'home alone' time, but it's really a case of what quality of life you intend to provide for your dog.

The outdoor kennel and run provides a safe, secure and comfortable environment for an adult dog and is the preferred choice of many owners who have to leave their dog alone for certain periods of the day. Unfortunately there are security issues that have to be considered as gundog theft continues at an alarming rate. So it's important to make kennels as secure as possible, to locate them discreetly and ideally to have a situation where a neighbour is within range should a dog be under any threat or distress. Kennels can now be easily fitted with alarm systems of various designs and while you may not be in a nearby position to react to such a warning, there may be someone close at hand who can. Hopefully once alarm devices are triggered they will make sufficient noise to deter an intruder.

Dogs left alone in the house are assumed to be less at risk from being stolen but in a domestic environment there can be more risk of a dog developing behavioural problems caused by sheer boredom. If a dog has to be left indoors for certain periods it's worth considering a cage – of ample size – as the best option. So while it's possible to own a working Labrador in a situation where the dog has to be left alone, make sure those periods are kept to a minimum.

## Day care

There are now plenty of opportunities to use the services of dog-carers during the day who will exercise a dog or spend some time with it and there are also kennels that offer day-time boarding. It's nevertheless important to remember that whoever provides help is fully aware of any training regimes you are undertaking. The last thing a working Labrador needs is a well meaning neighbour or dog-carer throwing a frisby around!

I would advise anyone who has thought their life-style to be unsuitable to owning a working Labrador to consider all the options and look closely at ways of overcoming any possible hurdles. Provided this is approached in a sensible and responsible manner and the dog's welfare is paramount, a workable system can often be devised.

The biggest issues arise when ownership begins with an eight-week-old pup – the most common start for most owners. Again, look at all the options well ahead of the time you make the decision to buy the pup. It may be that the breeder will keep the pup a little longer so that you feel you are more able to cope with a pup of say 12-weeks rather than eight weeks. Certainly just an extra month does make a big difference and you may feel more confident with a robust youngster to deal with.

## Travel

Being able to transport your dog safely by car is something that needs to be given plenty of consideration. There are practical issues – both in terms of the welfare of the dog, its safety and its security – that must be taken into account when looking at the options for providing a dog with the most suitable travelling arrangements. Whereas a straightforward dog guard in the back of an estate may still be adequate for some, it's far from ideal for a working gundog because a 'contained' space within the vehicle is preferable for all sorts of reasons. It helps to keep the car cleaner, it enables the dog to travel more securely and more comfortably and it means the dog can be left in the travelling box – with the door padlocked – when the rear door of the car is open and you need to leave the dog securely but without being totally locked inside the vehicle.

There are other issues to consider such as making sure the box is easily accessed from the front via an 'escape door' should anything untoward happen that means normal access to the box from the tailgate or rear door of the vehicle is prevented. It's important too to make sure the box is of solid construction and able to withstand any impact that the car may suffer if hit from behind and that it can be made totally secure if the dog has to be left inside the box when the rear door is open.

I am concerned that some travelling boxes seem very small for Labradors and while dogs do appear to have an ability to 'shrink' when put into a box, I don't think shoe-horning them inside has to be necessary. So make sure a box is big enough and high enough to provide a comfortable travelling space, that it's well ventilated, can be easily cleaned and also easily removed from the vehicle. And always consider the 'rattle factor' – there's nothing worse than a dog box that rattles from the moment you set off on your journey.

## Training equipment

There's now a plethora of suppliers of gundog training equipment offering an ever increasing range of dummies and gadgets to provide a vast selection to suit every stage of the dog's life and every level of ability.

To start with it's essential to have a whistle and lanyard and I prefer a 210.5 whistle. You should never have your dog out for training or exercise without having a whistle around your neck. Although small canvas puppy training dummies are available we rarely use them because by the time any meaningful retrieving work is underway a youngster can cope with a 0.5lb dummy. Initially a few 0.5lb canvas dummies will provide the basic tools for retriever training, later progressing to 1lb dummies. There are heavier

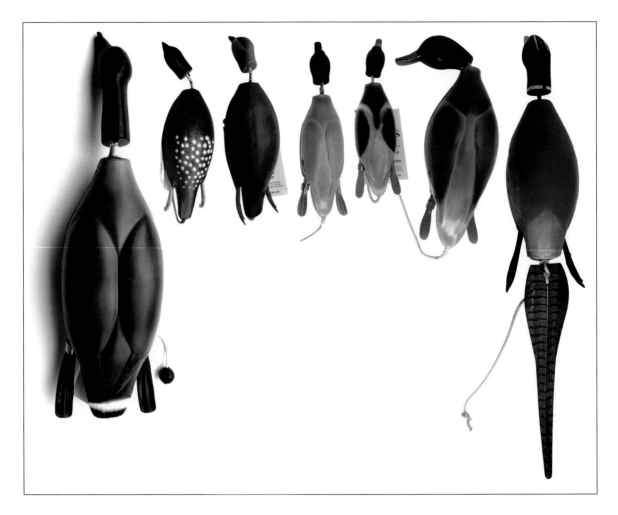

There is now a large range of training dummies and these rubber 'dead fowl trainers' are very useful *(Photo: Sporting Saint)*

weight dummies for the later stages which serve to emulate a hare in weight terms, while there are others that can help teach a dog how to balance heavier weights during a retrieve and can be useful if the dog is going to be used for wildfowling where geese will be an important part of the game bag.

To help the dog learn to be happy with the 'feel' of different textures in its mouth it's important to make use of tying rabbit skins and wing feathers to canvas dummies. The plastic game birds with 'wobbly heads' are also very useful and the plastic ducks – of various sizes – that float can be useful in water training.

The need to introduce the sound of 'shot' will require the purchase of a blank-firing pistol while a dummy launcher is an important part of the equipment for the later stages of training. A game bag needs to be big enough to carry comfortably a good selection of training equipment.

Recent years have seen canvas dummies available in a range of colours as well as dummies with tassels on them and other training dummies shaped like game birds, large eggs or small rugby balls. This expanding range of 'artificial' aids to teaching a dog how to retrieve may seem excessive and there are some who think that introducing too many different objects can have an adverse effect on a young dog's retrieving skills by making it hesitant at times or even leading to a tendency to 'mouth' during a retrieve. Personally I haven't encountered this and feel that many of the new training dummies make it easier to throw for the handler and broaden the dog's retrieving skills. If, however, you feel that any fault or issue is starting to develop which you believe may be attributable to the dummy or dummies you are using you should refrain immediately and return to those with which the dog feels more confident.

On the subject of colour I think there is some virtue in having a few brightly coloured dummies in the training bag to help raw youngsters 'see' a dummy rather than scent it in the early stages of training. And brightly coloured dummies are easier for the handler to find too! One thing I am a stickler about is for dummies to be kept as clean as possible. Left wet and covered in mud or other debris and then put back into the training bag

Canvas training dummies are now produced in a wide range of designs *(Photo: Sporting Saint)*

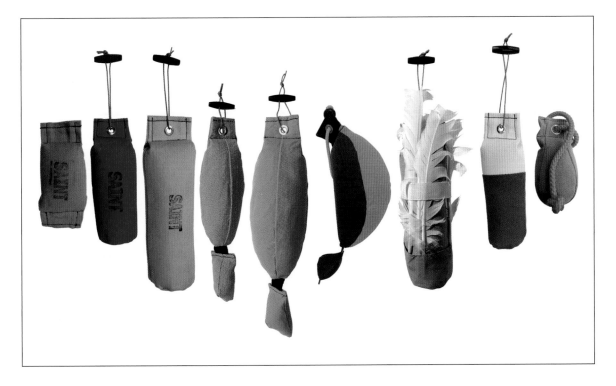

unwashed, produces canvas dummies that smell like sweaty socks. Because the nose and the mouth of the working Labrador are two very sensitive areas that we, as trainers, rely on very heavily to provide us with game retrieved swiftly, undamaged and not mouthed, I think it's important that the items we are asking young dogs to work with are as clean and untainted as possible. So a quick rinse under the tap after a training session and hung up to dry ensures all dummies are clean and fresh – and it's a standard that should be maintained even for dummies used for older dogs.

Help is always on hand for novice trainers through the training classes organised by local gundog clubs and via private trainers who hold individ-

Steady and ever-ready for work – a mature working-bred Labrador bitch

ual or group lessons. There is also the option of sending your young dog away to a professional trainer which may involve several sessions as the dog progresses. Some local gundog training classes are good and some not so good so it pays to either be recommended or go along first and make a judgement yourself. While there are many such classes run by good trainers not all acknowledge the wide diversity in terms of temperament and ability of the dogs and handlers under their instruction – so avoid a class that you feel doesn't follow your preferred approaches to training. And be careful not to end up in a training class that's driven by a working test ethic; all too often this attitude can turn a gundog training class into a lesson more suitable to collies being honed for obedience competitions.

The request to suggest a trainer who will 'train but not break' a young dog is often made by those who have had previous experience of a dog

*Always watching but never anticipating – steadiness at all stages of a shooting day is essential (Photo: Anne Taylor)*

Three working
Labradors, sitting
and ready to go

coming back to them after a period of training that was clearly a very different dog in terms of personality. So again, if your decision is to send a dog away to be trained either base your selection on a recommendation or visit some professional trainers and decide if you think their methods will benefit your dog and meet the standards you require.

•

# CHAPTER FOUR

# Rearing the Young Labrador and Achieving 'Connection'

T
HE FIRST SIX-MONTHS in the life of a Labrador are a critical period for both its physical and psychological development. What happens during this time will have a significant influence on the life-time health of the dog as well as its ability to move seamlessly into the 'teenage' stage and later into adulthood with a correct and well-balanced attitude to you as its owner, to its formative training and to its ultimate role as a working gundog.

I aim to make a 'connection' with my pups at this early stage. By connection I mean a union of communication and understanding between myself and the pup. Through this rudimentary awareness in the puppy my aim is to develop that early connection as the basis of all future training.

This is a very impressionable age for an intelligent working gundog, so before considering the step-by-step progression of rearing and management during this period in the pup's life, let's first take a look at the influences that have already been brought to bear on the pup up to the point at which it leaves its littermates.

It will be of considerable help to you as the pup's new owner to know as much about a pup's first eight weeks of life as possible. The pup should, of course, be no younger than eight weeks before it leaves the litter and in good health. Fortunately Labrador pups are fairly robust but that often means they survive poor conditions of rearing and yet still reach the eight-week stage. As a puppy buyer you must be fully satisfied that the litter has been reared to the highest standards – both nutritionally, environmentally and psychologically.

Set your standards high and don't buy a pup from a litter that is being reared in poor conditions. There are still some who adhere to the assumption that just because they are breeding 'working' gundogs it's acceptable for pups to tolerate the most basic of rearing standards. That is no longer appropriate. Pups that are poorly fed, badly housed and unsocialised – all in the name of 'working gundogs' – must be avoided at all costs.

Buying a pup from someone who is recommended to you or who is well known for the high standard of pups they breed is undoubtedly the preferred choice. Internet searches and phone calls will probably be the first points of contact with those who have pups for sale. A personal visit is always recommended to ascertain precisely who you are dealing with and to ensure they keep their dogs and rear their pups to the correct standards. Don't be too discouraged if a breeder refuses to let you see the pups in the

This 13-year-old bitch demonstrates the trust and confidence that lasts a lifetime

first few weeks after they have been born. Any responsible breeder doesn't want all and sundry visiting the kennels and increasing the risk of introducing unwanted disease to the vulnerable whelps – certainly for the first few weeks. So if you are requested to delay your initial inspection of the pups this is often the sign of a breeder who is extremely vigilant. Of course your eventual visit will enable you to make sure your first impressions of the breeder were correct and that the standard of rearing is as you expected. Take note too of the pups and their behaviour. Make sure they are lively and active and if there has been a radio on in the kennel so much the better because at least they will be used to some noise! It's easy to assess if pups have had plenty of time spent with them by noticing their responses to human interaction. Even at the six-weeks stage, the point at which you will probably be allowed your first inspection, they should be bold and outgoing if they've had ample human contact. It isn't unusual for some litters to rarely see people and hear voices apart from at feeding time – something that all too often sows the seeds of hesitancy and unpredictability in the developing youngster.

Before you agree to buy a pup you must see copies of all the relevant health certificates applicable to both the sire and dam. As a minimum these should cover hip scores (joint score of both hips to be no more than 15) and a current eye test result for both the sire and dam and dated within a year of the litter's birth. Ideally additional health screening information provided by the breeder should include elbow scores (0.0 is a perfect elbow score) as well as DNA test results for *prcd*PRA and centronuclear myopathy (CNM). The breeder should provide you with a puppy pack containing copies of all of these plus the pup's pedigree and hopefully a cover note providing four weeks insurance. Not all breeders will have completed the Kennel Club registration certificates by the day of collection so it isn't unusual to have this document sent to you later. You will of course then have to sign this document and return it to the Kennel Club to enable the 'official' transfer of ownership to be recorded. You will then receive another registration form from the Kennel Club which will show the pup has been transferred to your ownership.

New owners should receive a 'puppy pack' providing a very detailed description of the pup's feed requirements in terms of what diet is currently being fed, how much and how often. Ideally the breeder should provide a 'token' quantity of the puppy food to avoid any sudden change in diet. Make sure you discuss with the breeder the type of puppy food that has been used. You may decide to acquire the same or opt for your own choice. Whatever the decision any change to the pup's diet must be made gradually over the first two weeks.

Your pup should be bright and lively and showing no sign of nervousness or dullness of eye. The puppy information sheet should also tell you how many times the pup has been wormed since it was born. A pup needs to have been wormed at least three times before it leaves its littermates. As the new owner you need to know when the pup was last wormed and with what product. Likewise if the pup has been treated with any flea-compound you need to be aware of the treatment date and the product used. Some pups, not many, are sold having had the first part of their vaccination. If that's the case you will be provided with the certificate and must ensure the second and final part of the vaccination is undertaken by your own vet within the required time – usually two weeks from the first vaccination.

Although much depends on the time of year, you need to be aware of what form of heating had been provided for the litter. A pup taken from its littermates and from a kennel where there may also have been a heat lamp – at least at night – is certainly going to feel colder when required to sleep alone. Remembering the importance of minimising any trauma during transition from the breeder to you, this information is very relevant – or certainly will be if it avoids having to deal with a noisy, cold and unhappy puppy in the middle of the night!

The journey home with the pup needs to be made as easy as possible for all concerned. Pups confined to dog boxes in the rear of a vehicle usually end up being sick and probably whine and whinge for most of the journey. It means you arrive home with a distressed, wet, cold and disorientated pup – not the most auspicious start to your relationship or the best preparation for its new life and its first few hours away from everything it has ever known. If it's at all possible I advise that newly bought pups are either held – wrapped in a blanket or large towel – for the journey home or constrained in a dog-carrier placed on the rear seat and which can be easily accessed by an adjacent passenger. It pays to remember that the biggest and most traumatic change to this pup's life is its initial separation from its siblings. While young pups quickly adapt to their new found independence, subjecting them to unnecessary stress at the very outset is unwise when it can be so easily avoided. The aim should be to arrive home with a pup that feels secure and is as confident as it can be and not one that has had to endure enforced travel sickness.

Once home with the pup the routine that follows will depend upon where the pup is going to live. But wherever that may be the first job is to put the puppy somewhere to allow it to relieve itself. And when it 'performs' you must start as you mean to go on and lavish praise. Don't underestimate the value of this. Just think about all those occasions – say just before you compete at a test or a trial or any other situation that presents itself – when you need instant 'action' and you can get it on command. If a pup is always encouraged and learns a specific phrase or word, this part of house training – and even in adult life – can be a real advantage.

The early and most formative stages of a dog's life are extremely important to its mental and physical development. Unfortunately when corners are cut in terms of day to day management – albeit unintentionally – behavioural issues and even training problems can occur.

A new puppy purchased at around eight-weeks old requires plenty of time spent with it to help it become accustomed to its new surroundings and adjust to a new regime. So if you are planning on housing the pup in a kennel it's best to delay the move outside until the pup has settled. It's always important to remember that this is a dog with whom you are going to develop a very close working relationship and from the pup's point of view that relationship starts from day one. So take care to avoid any situations that could trigger hang-ups that may not emerge until formal training begins.

Only when the pup is settled and secure in its new environment should it be left – and for no more than four hours maximum – be that in a kennel or cage. Make sure the cage or crate is as large as possible. Although some attitudes to training believe long periods of confinement serve to build a strong bond between dog and owner, it's not a regime I subscribe to and for novice owners who feel such an approach to dog ownership fits in well with their work commitments, I would simply say that when adopted by inexperienced owners it is more likely to lead to problems than yield benefits.

So providing a pup or young dog is only left for short periods of the day there's no reason why owning and training a working gundog can't fit into a modern family lifestyle. The most important consideration is how you can best provide the care and attention the dog needs within the framework of your other commitments. The working Labrador's adaptability is legendary, so make the most of it, but don't abuse it.

## Crates and cages

Cages – or crates – have become part of modern dog ownership and while they serve a useful purpose in some respects, their use must be kept firmly in context. Cages for dogs kept in the house must be used sensibly and not excessively. It's important to avoid using a cage as a place where a pup or youngster is put purely for convenience rather than keeping the pup out of the cage and addressing whatever situation you are trying to avoid. If the cage is always used as an 'easy option' – when visitors call or at family meal-times – the pup will never learn how to behave correctly.

If the cage also provides the pup's sleeping place in the house it must regard it as a haven of safety and not somewhere used purely for confinement and solitude or where it is sent as a punishment. So ensure time spent in a cage is a 'happy time' so that the pup is accepting of it, is relaxed and not stressed. If you are intending to leave the pup in the cage when you go out it's advisable to start off with short periods undertaken while you are still in the house so that the pup doesn't assume the cage is only a place associated with being left alone.

Try feeding the pup in the cage or give it something to chew on while it's in there. This is all part of providing the pup with a good environment and positive experience rather than allowing the first few months of its life with you to be one of unpredictability. These approaches to gundog ownership are not, in essence, relevant to those who manage working gundogs in a kennel-based environment where the owner is able to spend plenty of time with the dogs, but aimed at one-dog novice owners embarking upon the rearing and training of a working Labrador for the first time.

The importance of adopting a correct management regime for a gundog pup hasn't received as much consideration in the past as it should have done, but as working gundogs must now adapt to modern life-styles it's essential that no problems are inadvertently allowed to develop at this important and highly influential stage.

Of course there will be times when a house-reared pup has the freedom of a larger part of the house and the question always arises; 'Can a working gundog be brought up as part of the family?' The answer is 'yes', provided some firm ground rules are established from the start.

A Labrador that has a future as a working gundog will be expected to do far more with its life than a Labrador bought purely as a pet, so it's important to remain constantly aware of all early influences, no matter how trivial they may seem at the time. A working Labrador reared in the house should never be chased around, no matter what it has done or what it's carrying in its mouth. It should never be allowed to chew anything that may in later life adversely affect it's retrieval of game. While hide chews, bones and hard rubber toys are fine, no soft toys that can be ripped apart must be given to the pup and a pup must never be allowed to chase and retrieve balls or children's toys in a play situation.

These may seem harsh rules and they may be rules that some families feel they cannot adhere to, but it has to be understood that the brain of a working Labrador begins operating from the day it's born and by the time you acquire an eight-week old pup its natural instincts are already very active. Yes, puppyish and silly they may be, but they are there and extremely acute nonetheless. Even a young pup will quickly pick-up bad habits. To expect a pup to forget all the things it has wrongly been allowed to do during the first eight months of life and suddenly become transformed into a diligent student at eight-months old and ready to learn is very naive. So from the very beginning, in everything that happens to the pup and in every experience it encounters, the owner must have a clear understanding of what expectations he or she has for the dog. Far better to avoid any undesirable influences in the pre-school stage rather than having to overcome them in a truculent youngster in training.

A pup that is to be kennelled should not be installed immediately. A transition time between house and kennel is essential so try making use of a spacious cage situated somewhere in the house that can be used to contain the pup when necessary but one that is nevertheless in a situation where the pup can see and hear all that is going on around it. Cages must not be used to confine the pup for long periods. An eight-week old pup may appear to have anything on its mind other than bonding with a new owner but the first few days are absolutely critical in establishing that early connection with the pup – a connection that will form the essence of your relationship and define how successful you are once formal training begins.

The first basics of formalised training can start at around eight months old

If the kennel is to be the ultimate home for the pup as an adult it's advisable to start achieving a positive association with the kennel as soon as possible. A young pup can look totally lost in a large kennel so be mindful of the situation. Feed the pup in the kennel and use it for any other occasions where a positive connection can be allowed to develop – a really hard chew bone can work wonders for 20 minutes! Remember you have a very intelligent pup on your hands. This is no lap-dog with no real purpose in life. This is a bright, sharp, intuitive pup that has been bred for a job. Even at this young age it will be using that intelligence at every opportunity to assess each situation that presents itself. That's why it's important not to underestimate the importance of these early times and the influences they will bring to bear in due course. A pup that has a traumatic start in its transitional time from litter to new owner is more likely to develop tendencies you don't want to have to start unravelling later. All this advice is not meant to pander to the pup and create a youngster that is molly-coddled and lacks confidence and spirit. It's intended to help build a confident pup that's happy in its surroundings, has a routine that re-creates the stability that nurtured it for the first eight weeks of its life and will be critical in shaping the foundation of your relationship. A pup that has been forced to undergo periods of re-adjustment involving any distress or confusion will be all the more difficult to train. A little care and consideration given to those first few weeks after leaving its fellow whelps should produce a bold and yet biddable pup by three-months-old and one that's devoid of the hang-ups that may not fully materialise until later.

## Puppy nutrition

An eight-week-old pup should be fed four meals a day. While there are various feed regimes that can be used most pups are reared on a complete diet that simply requires the addition of 'off the boil' water to produce a moistened feed. Some breeders still use meat – possibly minced tripe or beef fed with a biscuit meal – while others have adopted a natural approach to feeding based on raw meat, chicken wings or carcasses and vegetables.

Always use a high quality diet for rearing pups – although that doesn't necessarily mean the most expensive brands. Most complete diet puppy feeds are around 27% protein – considered necessary to provide a high level of dietary protein to meet the nutritional needs of a rapidly growing pup.

Some manufacturers are now introducing puppy feeds with a slightly lower protein content – around 24% – based on concerns expressed about prolonged feeding of higher levels of dietary protein once fast-growing pups of the bigger breeds, such as Labradors, develop beyond the 10-week stage.

Pups need three meals a day at three months-old reducing to two at six-months old. It's advisable to continue to feed pups on a puppy diet until around six months old and then to switch (gradually) to a 23% protein complete diet. Some manufacturers offer a specific 'junior' feed but a 23% protein complete diet of your preferred choice should be adequate.

Be mindful of the body condition of growing pups and don't be too rigid in quantities fed. All pups grow at different stages and, like humans, some burn up energy a lot faster than others. No pup should be allowed to get fat but I'd rather see growing pups well covered in order to have enough condition to meet their growth needs rather than see them kept leaner. Providing a pup isn't carrying excess weight that could be putting joints under pressure, it's easy to cut back and take condition off at the appropriate stage. Growth and development adversely affected by nutritional shortfalls in the critical stages of a young pup's life can never be recovered. So better to err on the side of slightly more in order the build the engine instead of less and suffer a breakdown.

## Forging a partnership

The brain of a young Labrador doesn't have a precise point at which it suddenly becomes receptive to training, but before anything can start to be learned by your dog it has to trust. Trust and confidence in you are the essence of a life-long partnership.

Doing all you can to achieve that must be a priority from the very earliest days of ownership. The ultimate aim should be to own a dog that works with you rather than for you. There will be many occasions when the knowledge, intelligence and intuition of your working Labrador will be greater than your own; when that situation arises you will be totally dependent on your dog's initiative and your dog must have the confidence in your relationship to apply it and not hesitate for fear of reprisal. Never forget you are forging a partnership – so make a friend of your partner. That may seem a somewhat simplistic comment to make in a book about working gundogs but the alternative is to go in the opposite direction and make an enemy of the dog. Interestingly enough you may not perceive yourself to be the enemy but unless a dog trusts you implicitly and you have complete faith in him, your relationship will always be problematic. How many times have we heard stories of young dogs that have apparently been cured of various training 'issues' only to suddenly exhibit some totally unexpected behaviour when it was assumed all the problems had been ironed out.

Connection is a union of communication and understanding

No dog gets everything right all of the time but many dogs are put under too much pressure by novice trainers in the early stages. Yes, some young dogs are very challenging and it has become commonplace to apply severe standards in an effort to achieve the results. But fear-based methods don't create a foundation of trust between dog and handler and inevitably the fragility of the relationship will be its downfall. This situation is often perceived by the handler as an unmistakable show of defiance by the dog and what follows is usually an even more severe correction. The dog once again succumbs to the dominance of the handler but eventually that demonstration of unexpected behaviour will happen again. Dogs aren't infallible and even adopting a positive approach to training rather than a negative one will never mean a dog doesn't do something out of the ordinary. But dogs treated fairly in their training will demonstrate fewer 'blips'; they will occur less frequently and with the appropriate approach to correction and re-training they will eventually be cured.

In a future chapter we will be looking in more detail at the importance of voice communication as a training aid but before the pup's formal training begins there are real benefits to establishing responses and acknowledgement from the pup simply through the use of the voice. Pups will quickly learn to be extremely attentive to the human voice and yet even though we will be looking for a very acute level of response to our voice when formal training begins, many owners fail to recognise the value of the human voice in the early stages of the pup's life. So at this point suffice to say that talking to the pup – and I mean far more than simply using its name – will create an instant line of communication that will prove invaluable as the pup matures.

## Puppy exercise

If I retain a single pup from a litter I always re-unite the pup with its dam after the rest of the littermates have left. I don't like kennelling a pup on its own so 'bunking-up' with mum again is no bad thing. If I keep two pups from a litter I'll kennel them together. A working dog should have a long and active life so I am in no rush to do anything with pups apart from let them see and learn as much as they can in and around the kennels. Leads and puppy dummies don't factor into any of it during the early stages. I'm very careful about exercise and from experience believe it's important to allow pups to have some freedom to help in the correct development of limbs and joints but not too much that could risk any damage.

Labrador pups love to charge about and, if they have been kennelled or in the house they will bound about recklessly when given freedom. I never allow pups to even play with older dogs, simply because the 'rough and tumble' play with an adult can cause pups to twist and contort themselves and play chasing games they will never win – all this does is increase the pressure on developing joints and is best avoided. So the main rules for puppy exercise – and this is up to the age of six months – is to let it happen in an area over which you have control (garden, paddock or other enclosed space), always be aware of how much time pups have for this sort of playtime and restrict it rather than allow pups to get exhausted. Always (if the pup is being exercised alone) let the pup make all the running in terms of what it wants or does not want to do.

It's unwise to turn a pup out into the garden or into a paddock and leave it there for half and hour. I always closely monitor how much time pups have to play freely and believe time spent with them – say just 10-minutes at a session several times a day – not only enables the first stages of 'connection' to become established but gives you the opportunity to

Start to develop a pup's instinct for hunting at an early stage and as part of the pup's playtime

assess pups, what they get up to during play and how they respond to different play situations.

During these 'play' times there's no need to over-stimulate the pup, to chase it or make it do more than it wants to do. The pup knows its own limitations and provided none of the exercise it undertakes is enforced in any way, its physical development should be unchallenged. Too little freedom (in a controlled space) is as bad as too much (in an open space).

Like children, modern-day pups are more advanced at a younger age and grow faster because of improved genetics and nutrition. So to put things in perspective it's useful to look at the size of an eight-week-old pup and imagine what size it's going to reach over the next 16 weeks. While it won't reach full adult size by that stage it will rapidly be heading that way – and that's a phenomenal amount of development in a short time. To support that rate of physical progress the limbs and joints are under considerable pressure and soft tissue can easily be damaged. So as well as closely monitoring exercise, a pup must not be allowed to jump up over things or jump off things – both actions apply undue press to developing joints.

## Training – when to start

'When should training start?' – is without doubt the question most asked by those about to embark upon training their first working Labrador. But the real question is how to define 'training'? Education is probably a better word to use when referring to pups under seven months old because they require more in terms of education rather than actual training. There are successful trainers who adopt a very early start to formal training and have heelwork underway at four months and even younger; and there are others who prefer to leave pups completely alone until nine or ten months. There is a half-way house, a way of educating and teaching a pup to be responsive and attentive to you without actually starting any formal training until say seven or eight months old. That's the way I like to do it.

In many cases lead training is started far too early creating tension between dog and handler. Putting a lead on a dog as soon as possible is often the first thing novice owners think they have to do. It's as though the lead gives a clear, but obviously incorrect, message to the dog that the owner has now gained control. In effect it creates a pressure point and

inevitably means the relationship gets off on the wrong foot. The owner is trying to impose control over an exuberant and playful pup; you want control, you want to achieve that magic thing called 'heeling' and you set off at a brisk pace uttering the 'heel' mantra which means nothing at all to the pup. There follows the inevitable jerking and dragging it back as the pup pulls forward. You jerk, the pup pulls, you get frustrated, the pup lies down or chokes on the lead and you very quickly have a whole raft of issues developing that you didn't envisage. None of this would have happened if you had delayed your lead training until you had 'connection' or at least a better relationship with the pup.

Early training should be undertaken in a very casual way with no formal sessions, just an on-going positive attitude to the way in which the pup is managed in all things.

Dogs do not comprehend human language *per se*, only sounds that we want them to associate with certain actions. But the human voice is an

Total and utter faith in you is the ultimate goal

invaluable education tool when dealing with all dogs – and pups in particular. I talk a lot when I'm in the kennels; it ensures all the dogs are always listening and attentive to my voice and are constantly aware of me and what I am doing. I am cheerful and bright and maintain a positive attitude but, should the dogs create a situation I am not happy about, I only have to lower the tone of my voice to get an instant response and a clear behavioural acknowledgment from them that they have picked-up on my displeasure. No need to shout, no need to yell, just lower the tone and watch the response. It's instant.

I like to keep very light-hearted and cheery when I'm dealing with pups of any age. I want to engender trust and 'connection' from the start. This is the beginning of what will hopefully be a long relationship and a friendship has to be established. When you see pups that drop their ears and back off to the other side of the kennel it's clearly a sign they've been chastised far too severely for something and are now unsure of where they are in the relationship. It engenders weak bonds for future training as well as underlying mistrust – the last thing anyone wants in a dog where total and utter faith and belief in you is the ultimate goal.

So lots of praise and confident chatter is what I dish out to pups in bucket-loads. There may be days when all sorts of things can be adding to the pressures of life but I always maintain a light-hearted attitude to youngsters.

Whenever I am with pups in the paddock I always have a whistle around my neck and a few nuggets or cubes of dog food or small dog biscuits in a pocket – two essentials to help build the connection with growing youngsters. At play I call pups back to me regularly and give an appropriate reward and pile on the praise. The call is gradually replaced with the whistle and every time I get the desired response a reward and praise is given. I don't overplay this and am mindful that if a pup is totally pre-occupied with something and I feel a call or a whistle may fall on deaf ears, I wait. All of these early pieces of education are intended to achieve a positive response. The aim is to get the pup to succeed every time.

I am never in a rush to get a lead around a pup's neck. Do it too soon and it can turn into a totally unnecessary and avoidable tug of war. The handler wants to go one way and the pup resists. It's too young to grasp precisely what you are trying to make it do and the whole affair ends up giving a negative result and probably means there will be more problems later.

I may decide to try a lead on a pup at about five months old but for the most part I don't bother trying any lead training until much later – say six or seven months. Walking at heel is always seen as the big stepping stone to training. It's not. I like to have a pup following me at heel without a lead before I want the same level of attentiveness with a lead on. Provided it's undertaken at the right moment, I can have a pup walking at heel in just a few minutes because the pup feels safe with me and it wants to be with me – and following me seems a much better option than being left behind!

With a few treats to keep the focus of concentration on me rather than thinking too much about resisting – as well as loads of encouragement – I can achieve good heel work in minutes.

Teaching a pup to walk at heel too soon can cause all sorts of issues when it has to be achieved by force. And by applying unnecessary pressure on the pup to achieve this degree of control can have a negative impact on other things. I often see heelwork being almost manically trained to the point at which it can take the youthful enthusiasm out of a pup. The strict obedience-style approaches that some training clubs base their methods

Never forget you are forging a partnership – so make a best friend of your partner (*Photo: Sharon Rogers*)

I like to have a pup following me at heel without a lead before I look for the same level of attentiveness on the lead

around can, and often do, take all the 'fizz' out of gundog pups. So avoid getting caught up in training programmes that seem more focussed on promoting 'circus tricks' and concentrate more on nurturing natural ability.

Hunting with gusto, being able to stop and take commands from the handler and being steady and focussed on the handler at all times are the key elements of an effective working Labrador. Retrieving and walking to heel are important skills that have to be learnt but Poodles in the park will retrieve and any mongrel can be taught to walk to heel so these two parts of training need to be taken in context. They can both be mastered in stages and should not be drilled into the dog mercilessly.

A great deal of time seems to be spent trying to perfect these copy-book exercises with the assumption that once a certain level has been achieved, the dog has been given a perfect grounding for all that is to follow. Not so.

I like to start to develop a pup's instinct for hunting at an early stage as part of the pup's play time. By hiding a small object – possibly something the pup is familiar with – in long grass or behind a bush, and encouraging the pup to hunt for it, is as satisfying for the handler as it is for the pup when there's a successful outcome. As I play this game I start to progress it by catching the pup's attention and encouraging it to move a few feet across a certain area using my hands. I will start to bring in the whistle to this game giving a sharp pip as the pup looks up and then re-directing with my hand to encourage searching a new area close by.

This is a time when pups have unbridled enthusiasm for all that they do and as an adult dog this is what life is going to be about – finding game. So often pups that have been subjected to endless square bashing to perfect heel work and then had steadiness exercises taken to the point where the pup seems almost bored, often finish up being too 'hot' when allowed to let their hair down and asked to hunt or are so worried by this sudden permitted freedom, that they are not committed enough in their hunting skills and seem hesitant and unconfident.

Many of the problems encountered once formal training commences can be attributed to owners not having nurtured a close rapport with their pups during the first few months. This is a critical time that should be used to establish the all-important basic connections between pup and owner. Although referred to as 'informal training' it can be as simple as making sure the pup learns to listen to you and respond to you. These are the foundations of links in your relationship that will prove invaluable and can be of huge benefit later.

Confusion and resistance are attitudes towards training characterised by pups whose owners mistakenly believe all will eventually 'fall into place' as the pup matures – based on the assumption that they have a working Labrador whose natural ability can easily be tapped into once formal training begins.

Every pup is an individual and there is no single approach to training that can be applied to every dog with the intention of achieving a well-trained gundog. As a guide I would say the first basics of formalised training can start at around eight months old – but that is very much a rule of thumb. However no pup should be spending all the time up to that point simply being fed and allowed some exercise. Every day is a training day – but keep it subtle and low-key. The intention should be to forge a relationship in a way that following signs, instructions and commands becomes a totally natural way of behaviour for the pup.

Always remember that 'instruction will not be understood without connection' and where problems do occur it's because there is little or no true connection between dog and owner. If total obedience and the desire to obey at all costs is the ultimate aim of the relationship you have with your dog it's a very insecure basis for a successful partnership. The primary aim in the early stage of the pup's life – apart from caring for its essential needs – is to forge a connection of understanding. Some may call it a bond but it's actually far more than that. Your playful, four-month-old pup if it were living as a wild dog, would be learning a great deal at that age. It would be learning from its parents – in other words its mentors. It wouldn't be left to turn into an unruly adolescent and then taken on one side at nine-months-old and given the handbook of life. But that's what happens all too often with young working Labradors. The transition between puppyhood and the start of formal training should be seamless provided you have created the correct level of connection. Your dog should be totally 'in tune' with you by the time it's six months old and by that stage you should confidently be able to 'read' the dog in terms of its behaviour and responses. This degree of mutual understanding and awareness can only be achieved if you allow the 'connection' to fully develop.

So don't pressurise the pup during the first six months but equally don't let it become a rampaging hooligan that knows no parameters of what it should and shouldn't do. A pup in the first six months of life must be respectful; it needs to have manners and you need to establish control. The level of control you can achieve by this stage often surprises people because they assume that control can only be gained by forcing a pup to do what you are imposing upon it and chastising it when it fails to deliver the anticipated response. Control during the first six months can be achieved without any undue pressure; it must be encouraged and developed by voice commands, by visual aids and by body language – all providing essential signs and signals that a pup will respond to. It's about building a mutual awareness and about a mutual trust.

Young, growing Labradors won't learn very much cooped up in a kennel for hours on end; equally excessive exercise – all too often given to a youngster as a means of 'taking some of the steam off' – will not only cause damage to soft tissue in developing joints but will simply serve to heighten the level of uncontrolled behaviour even though it may result in a biddability falsely induced by tiredness.

## Puppy play school

Exercise for youngsters needs careful monitoring. Today's well-bred and well-reared Labradors grow much faster than they did 40 years ago so damage to developing joints is an increasing risk which can lead to problems, particularly with elbows. So while it's essential to allow pups to have some freedom, it has to be controlled. While there was a period of time when keeping pups in a restricted environment and allowing minimum freedom was considered necessary to avoid 'puppy lameness' – a term often used to describe the elbow condition osteo-chondritis – veterinary advice now suggests it's important to allow controlled free running for short periods to enable the correct muscular development without putting joints under too much strain. I allow pups to have supervised freedom for short periods and never exercise growing pups with older dogs. The inevitable always happens and the older dogs set the pace that the pups try to match.

Control exercise in terms of the time allocated and the area in which they have to play.

Always remember that instruction will not be understood without connection

I always maintain voice contact with pups, even when they are playing and never stand by in total silence. The idea is to make sure the pup continues to keep 'one ear cocked' for anything I might say, usually on the basis that it may well be to its advantage. But for whatever reason it ensures the pup develops an awareness of your voice and learns that it has to maintain that awareness even though it may appear to be totally pre-occupied doing something else.

You may not realise it but even though a pup may seem to be totally absorbed by a new smell or some other intriguing discovery, it will still know precisely where you are and be very aware of your presence. In these situations it's useful to strike a balance between allowing the pup to explore and learn, but from time to time giving a few encouraging pips on the whistle to ask the pup to come back to you. A positive response deserves a treat. What you've actually instigated by doing that is the very basics of the recall; the pup doesn't know it but it has learnt something already. Yes, it may be sloppy and uncontrolled and yes the pup probably will go around the back of you or jump up at you but that doesn't matter. These are foundations of connection and partnership. If the pup doesn't respond to the whistle you should stop blowing it. It's important not to persist when there is clearly an issue of failing to respond. The aim must always be to achieve a positive response so wait a few seconds and then blow again. If there's still no response, turn and walk away slowly. Invariably the pup will be well aware of what's happened and follow. At that point give a pip on the whistle as though everything was as it should have been had the response been immediate.

Of course this is all in informal 'play-mode' and very unpressured and relaxed but over a period of time try to gradually encourage the pup to come in front of you rather than go behind you. The old trick of standing against a wall is always successful. Over time you can start to give a pip on the whistle when the pup comes to you and gradually you may be able to achieve a sit position. Some pups do this easily, some less so but I find that with perseverance and patience I can have a pup of say five months old coming to me and being sufficiently steady to allow me to give a slightly longer and persistent pip on the whistle, raise a hand and achieve a sit. It will probably be very unco-ordinated and you may wonder what it's achieving, but if these exercises are undertaken in a relaxed and relatively unstructured way – almost as part of the pup's play time – you will be surprised by the results.

This isn't a way of enforcing any strong will on the pup but a method of forging links of response and hopefully developing a level of attentiveness and rapport that is fundamental and yet raw.

## Lead training – for real

There comes a time when walking correctly on a lead has to be learnt, but many approaches to lead training often create problems that didn't exist previously and usually mean this simple and basic piece of instruction takes far longer to master than is actually necessary. There are far more effective methods for achieving good heelwork that don't involve constant jerking and dragging back into position.

The aim should be for a dog to walk at heel because it knows that's where you want it to walk, not because it's afraid that if it doesn't there will be some form of correction applied. Correct heelwork is a delight to see; Labradors that creep along glued to the handler's knee with a fearful look in their eye are a very sad sight.

So how do you achieve good heelwork? Don't attempt to put a lead on a pup until it's probably at least five months old. Try it much before then and all the antics mentioned earlier will result and the inevitable battle of wills will ensue. The reason is simple – the pup is too young to understand what's wanted and too full of life to want to be easily restrained without resistance. I can have one of my own youngsters walking nicely to heel and even sitting when I stop within 15 minutes or less of putting a lead on, primarily because I have developed a relationship and connection with that pup that is not born out of fear but out of a partnership.

So what are the key principles of achieving good heelwork swiftly, calmly and without any stress on the pup? Find somewhere without distractions and pop a lead on the pup. By the time I do this – and because I know I'm not going to get a dog that tries to strangle itself as soon as the lead goes around its neck – I use a slip lead but it may be that others find it more appropriate to use a collar and lead just in-case things don't go according to plan and the tightening of a slip will only cause discomfort.

The assumption that the tighter a lead goes around a pup's neck the more control the handler has and the more readily the pup will learn to obey the constant demand to 'heel', is incorrect. With the lead on the pup start to move forward giving lots of encouragement and always have a

The ultimate aim should be a dog that works with you rather than for you *(Photo: Sharon Rogers)*

biscuit or treat in the hand to coax a forward motion. Yes, you may have to be very flexible as the pup does a few leaps and darts here and there for a few strides but with constant talking, coaxing and encouragement – and never allowing the pup to lose concentration – you should soon be walking forward with the pup walking along with you. The secret is not to walk too far but to turn and go in another direction, always maintaining the attention and giving ample praise and encouragement. This is a game, a light-hearted exercise with treats along the way. Keep the pup's attention, rattle treats or biscuits in your pocket and don't be afraid to get down to a level that's nearer to the pup to keep the forward momentum. The pup doesn't know what it's doing but it's walking alongside you because it wants to; unforced, unstressed and happy to do so. But don't labour this; just a few minutes of success is all you need for the first lesson. If you have achieved the desired 'connection' with your pup – and the pup's focus on you is borne out of positivity and the praise that has been established over a period of time –you should be able to stop, hold up a hand, give a long pip on the whistle and achieve a sit. That may seem too much to ask for some pups but if the groundwork has been done properly it can very often be an automatic response. I always feel that when that happens and a pup looks up at you and asks the question with its eyes 'was that OK?' – you are well and truly on the way to success in all that will follow.

If lead training and those very first few attempts to get a pup to walk alongside you are smattered with yells of 'heel' and lots of jerks and pulls, you are simply setting an agenda of conflict. This attitude sends a clear message to the pup that you are determined to enforce your will over his to achieve the required results. Compromise and co-operation are sadly lacking in this scenario. While some trainers or dog-breakers may wish to use these methods, many others – and in particular those training a dog for the first time – will achieve success more swiftly and in a way that's hugely beneficial to the pup through cooperation. Creating conflict from the outset – and heelwork is very often seen as the first stage of training and all too often the most contentious – simply means that every time a new stage in training is reached the dog knows the battle lines have been drawn and confrontation between dog and handler becomes more intense. Inevitably the methods required to achieve the desired results as training progresses become more severe as the dog becomes 'harder' and more resolute in its attitude.

## Feeding a pup

A Labrador pup at eight weeks old should be eating four meals a day – breakfast, lunch, late afternoon and late evening. You should hopefully have already obtained details about the food the litter has been reared on from the breeder so that you can continue with the same feed – at least for the first few days. If you have decided to change the diet this must be done very gradually although quite often it's the pup that can trigger a change! Very often a pup that has been a voracious feeder in a litter situation will suddenly go off its food when taken into a new environment. The causes are

You must be fully satisfied that the litter has been reared to the highest standards – nutritionally, environmentally and psychologically (*Photo: Anne Taylor*)

either a change in the taste caused by different water being used to moisten the food, a reaction to new surroundings or most likely that the competition that was guaranteed to encourage good feed intake in a litter situation has now been removed. The stimulus to eat – or miss out on a meal – has gone. In this situation the introduction of your preferred choice of food may be the solution. Try mixing the new feed with a little of the original diet to start with and very gradually make the change-over.

Rearing pups is one of the most satisfying jobs for a breeder and I believe no time nor cost nor effort should be spared. The first solid food I offer to pups at around three weeks old is liquidised Skinners Complete Puppy Food. We soak it with boiled water, then liquidise with a little goat's milk added. It provides all the nutrition a pup needs – even at this tender age with top-ups from mum. If you have total confidence in a top quality puppy food it will do a better job nutritionally than trying to rear a litter on a range of foods when in actual fact you aren't always certain of the true feed value. My pups stay on the same puppy diet until they leave at eight-weeks old. I always recommend pups are maintained on this diet until six-months-old.

# CHAPTER FIVE

·

# The Formative Year

I'M WELL KNOWN FOR using the phrase 'just let it be' when referring to my approach to the first few months of a young Labrador's life. So what does it mean and why do I believe it's so important?

Firstly, I'm not suggesting that a young Labrador should be left to its own devices during this period – and by that I mean reared without any effort on the part of the owner to influence its behaviour. Far from it. These early weeks are critical and have a big part to play in helping to develop the correct attitude, response and the all important connection.

Working Labradors spend a good deal of their first two years of life on a learning curve and there are certain stages when youngsters are expected to progress quite rapidly. Experienced trainers all have their own approaches to the way they deal with the 'pre-school' period – a time before any formal training begins in earnest. For new owners training a working Labrador for the first time, the puppy stage can often be the most daunting. It's demanding in terms of time because the pup tends to have a mischievous unpredictability about its behaviour and there's always the fear that it may pick up bad habits unless constantly corrected. There's a desire by many owners to start to control excessive unruliness and exuberance and to adopt basic training exercises – such as to sit and to stay – in the belief that this level of learning must be instigated from a very young age in order to lay the

The very essence of a gundog's role in life is to find and retrieve

foundations for easier training later on. But in novice hands this approach can all too often have the very opposite effect. Too much formality too soon – applied by an over-zealous owner with the best of intentions – creates confusion in the early stages and then later rebellion as confidence in the pup increases. And because of immaturity and a lack of comprehension of what's required the inevitable occurs and a battle of wills between dog and handler ensues.

Before we examine this 'pre-school' stage in more detail – a stage in a dog's life that cannot be underestimated in terms of the significance it has on all manner of behaviour and training as the dog matures – it's necessary to consider the advice often given to novices which advocates a very strict regime during this period. Such regimes are based on instilling a clear focus in the pup about what its role in life is going to be. It's a 'no nonsense' approach. The aim is to develop a clear understanding in the pup's mind that when it's out of the kennel its job is purely to learn its craft. Some methods recommend that owners only have any contact with their dogs during training sessions, that youngsters aren't allowed any 'play time' and that young dogs are only spoken to when given training commands.

Extreme you may say and I would certainly agree, but they are nevertheless in use and are recommended to novices by some trainers.

The main issue, and one that to me is so often over-looked, is that many novices neither want to adopt such extreme methods or certainly lack sufficient experience to implement them. When they attempt to apply them they often end up struggling with all sorts of training issues because these methods are a psychological approach to training that can so easily back-fire.

The matter of the appropriate level of discipline for dogs in training is often a topic of discussion among first-time owners of working Labradors. Inexperienced owners resort to applying varying degrees of physical discipline to their dogs in a vain effort to overcome a training problem. Physical discipline is somehow expected to convey to the dog the owner's displeasure at something it has done on the assumption that the dog will understand what has happened and refrain from repeating the mistake or risk further similar corrective action.

Heavy handedness in training gundogs is inappropriate and even some gundog training classes allow handlers to be excessive in their disciplinary measures. When applied by novices as a means of corrective action such measures inevitably trigger a downward spiral in the relationship between dog and owner and any hope of securing that vital connection is lost. There should be no need to use any form of physical discipline on youngsters as part of the learning process if the relationship and appropriate level of 'connection' has already been established. If a young dog is totally in-tune with the handler it should be sufficient to admonish, where necessary, with a stern word.

So let's examine a regime for training a working Labrador that can be applied from the earliest stages of puppyhood by new or relatively inexperienced owners and one that will seek to build and establish a mutual rapport and respect. If this can be achieved – and in so doing avoid the 'car crash' that is so often the result of an incorrect approach to the 'pre-school' period – it will engender a new found confidence among aspiring trainers rather than the inevitable struggle for supremacy between them and their dog.

Any pups I retain from a litter are put under no training pressure whatsoever until around seven to eight months old – but that isn't to say that they aren't learning before they reach this stage. If it's a single pup that's retained once all its littermates have left it will be returned to its dam and

While it may be boring to keep practicising the same 'tune' over and over again it will sound all the more sweeter the longer you do so

they will share a kennel. I don't isolate pups, so if there are two retained they will be kennelled together. It's an interesting topic of debate – one pup or two. I don't have any strict policy on that decision, it just depends what I feel we want to keep or run on for a while. I wouldn't advise anyone to go out and buy two pups on the basis that they will be company for each other. For the novice I would always advise buying one pup.

I operate an approach to rearing pups that allows them to come out of their kennel several times a day. I want pups to see and experience as much as they can but they are not restrained by a lead. While I may slip a lead on briefly at some stage if necessary, no proper lead training is undertaken until at least six-months old and possibly even later. Whether it's a collar or a slip lead, both will create friction and tension when applied to a pup that's too young. There is nothing to be gained by it. The pup wants to go one way, the handler wants to go in a straight line. The situation degenerates and by embarking upon even this basic bit of training you have introduced tension into your relationship when there was no real need to do so. Applied too early and the typical puppy tantrum that you have to overcome will have become the first clear indication of conflict between you and the pup. Not a good start to the long-term training relationship.

A well-balanced pup that's used to being with you and is old enough to have the basic understanding of wanting to work – primarily because you have connected with it and are already seen as 'the good guy' – can be taught to walk at heel within minutes if the timing of this early training is right. No pulling, no tantrums, no resistance.

The pre-school months can be the most valuable in forging bonds of mutual respect and confidence

## Early education

It's a daunting experience for a pup when it has to leave its littermates and while there is an assumption that because pups are full of fun they are oblivious to anything that falls outside the need to play, eat and sleep, in actual fact they are also learning to survive and to create quickly new associations with which they feel secure. Coming up to you for attention is a primary behavioural signal from the pup that it wants to forge that association and connection and such approaches must be encouraged.

The very essence of a gundog's role in life is to find and retrieve game. Returning game proudly to its owner and to meet with approval for a job well done completes the circle of the dog's existence. But delivering game to hand correctly and efficiently is an important skill that some dogs have naturally while others are less adept. So just as it's important not to throw balls or toys for pups to retrieve as part of any time spent playing with a pup or a youngster, care must be taken not to inadvertently express any resistance to the pup when it comes up to you for attention. No one wants even a young puppy persistently jumping up and creating a nuisance of itself, but care needs to be taken to avoid any corrective training in this regard that may inadvertently dissuade the pup from returning to you with gusto when retrieving training begins. Dogs that stand a yard off from the handler and hold the dummy; those that stand off from the handler and drop the dummy; those that don't retrieve correctly at all and those that run around the handler in circles, are all symptoms of corrective measures employed by the handler, albeit inadvertently, before training began.

The habit of jumping up at the handler should always be tackled in a way that isn't going to send a message to the dog that coming 'up close and personal' is unacceptable. So adopt a calm, precise and positive response and instead of pushing the dog away in an abrupt manner it's far better to place both hands on either shoulder of the dog to put it back in the standing or sitting position giving the command 'No'.

To make sure I encourage young pups to learn to come 'into my space' from being very young – and to come in very close – I sit down on the floor with my legs wide apart and call pups into the V-shape my position has created. This welcoming funnel never fails to attract young pups and I encourage them to come right up to me, even up to my chest if that's what they want to do when they are small. It's all part of developing the close connection from the earliest stages rather than putting up barriers and demarcation zones which can cause issues at a later stage.

All the time I'm dealing with pups in kennels or when they are allowed out for exercise they are being talked to. I maintain a high level of communication with all the dogs in the kennel and pups in particular; it's something that has always been part of the way I manage dogs. Pups benefit from hearing the human voice from an early age and it engenders an awareness that will become all the more important in later training. I don't simply speak when dealing with the pups individually but almost maintain a running commentary of what I'm doing while in the kennels. It's surprising how pups – and even adult dogs – are constantly aware of my voice and listening. It helps them develop an acute sense of sound and pitch. No kennel jobs are undertaken in silence. The on-going level of communication keeps dogs ever watchful and interested. I capitalise on this 'listening ability' more and more as dogs move through their training. It achieves faster responses to commands but it also enables me to impart displeasure swiftly and effectively simply by changing the tone. Likewise I can effectively express delight and approval for a job well done.

Focus on achieving a pup that watches your every move, that daren't take its eyes off you in case it misses something good

So when I have a pup or pups out with me in the exercise paddock I'm talking constantly to maintain contact and to make sure they need to keep listening to me just in case they might miss something good! I always have a handful of dry dog food in a pocket so that when they come back to me they get a reward. While some advocate no whistle until formal training begins, once pups get to the three-month stage or thereabouts and are becoming more attentive rather than simply puppyish in their behaviour, I'll give 'two pips' to bring a pup up to me during this casual play time period. Depending on the pup and how receptive it is I may even hold up a hand to see if the pup will sit without any coercion. Although playful pups are unlikely to respond to this at first it's surprising how there suddenly comes a stage when I do get a response and the pup will sit. This doesn't indicate the start of any formal training, it's simply a point at which there is beginning to be some connection with the pup. What you have actually achieved is a recall, a sit and possibly even a 'short stay' – the pup isn't aware of what it has done, it's all been undertaken without any formality on your part but here are the very first signs of co-operation and connection that will prove invaluable as time progresses.

Obviously no balls are thrown, there's no chasing and no silly antics that may undermine what we will be moving onto later in terms of training. My pups are allowed and encouraged to investigate and explore, but there's always someone just a few yards away. By constantly talking to them and giving verbal encouragement makes sure pups always have one ear open to whatever you may be saying, even though the pup may appear to be completely pre-occupied.

My hands are as important to me as my voice in these 'pre-school' months. Whether you aspire to field trials, simply need a good peg-dog or are happy to enjoy your Labrador in the picking-up team on the local shoot, your hands and the signals they send will be critical as a means of communication. I have to admit that I wasn't fully aware of how much my dogs watch my hands until several years ago when someone who came to me for a training session made a comment while we were moving some dogs around the kennels that 'your dogs never take their eyes off your hands'. Ever since then I have become more aware of something that I had developed unconsciously over 30 years of dealing with dogs – and yes I do use my hands far more than I realised. I guide dogs in and out of kennels with hands, I use my hands as a vital part of all my training – in fact anywhere I want dogs to go or have some instruction to give I use my hands just as much as I use my voice.

If you can establish this awareness and recognition of hands as an extension of your voice from an early stage, pups certainly do respond extremely positively. Hands can become almost like a magnet as well as a method of guidance and direction once dogs begin to recognise the significance and the movement of hands in terms of communication. The raised hand with the palm flat as a signal for stop or sit is a fundamental part of training but I can confidently say that if a pup becomes so used to watching your hands and using them as an indicator of what you want it to do you will be amazed at what can be achieved.

Pushing a dog's hindquarters down and repeatedly saying 'sit' is considered the most effective approach to achieving this position. But if a pup is attentive and responsive enough to the hands of the owner, it should only take a raise of the hand and possibly just a whisper of 'sit' to achieve

It's vital to maintain the enjoyment and enthusiasm in youngsters (*Photo: Anne Taylor*)

what's wanted. Let's never forget how intuitive these dogs are and if these methods are applied at the right stage in the pup's life and regularly re-inforced – and to pups that are eager to learn – rather than determined to be obstreperous – the positive results will speak for themselves.

The premise that 'a dog should work with you and not for you' high-lights the importance of creating a partnership founded on trust and a genuine and unquestioning willingness to please rather than a relationship of total subservience. Creating a partnership is fundamental to getting the best out of your dog, but partnerships are based on communication and connection; if one side of the partnership fails to tell the other what's hap-pening there's an immediate breakdown in that communication and co-operation is lost. That's why a breakdown in communication is so often the root cause of many problems in potentially good partnerships between working Labradors and their owners. The dog is often unsure about what it's required to do and it's not simply because the handler has failed in his or her execution of the recommended training procedures. Very often the relationship between dog and handler isn't as good as it should be and imparting information is never easy when lines of communication have been severed. Many novice handlers become frustrated because they believe they have followed training instructions implicitly, been advised by trainers, read books and watched videos, but still the dog fails to progress or persists in undertaking a task incorrectly. When these 'blips' occur there's often recourse to imposing discipline as a means of correction when it simply exacerbates the situation. It doesn't make the dog learn any faster it just adds another layer of confusion to a situation that is awash with mixed messages. What was an issue that could have been dealt with relatively easily suddenly becomes something far greater than it should be.

Novice trainers can make real progress if they are prepared to give just a little more time for their dogs to assimilate instruction and resist the back-lash of information overload. Intelligence and intuition go hand-in-hand in the way a young Labrador learns its craft but lay the building bricks of learning very carefully and slowly.

No one can deny that watching experienced and well-trained Labra-dors responding to accomplished handling is a joy, but the responsive atti-tude that we admire so much in these dogs can be achieved to a lesser but equally effective degree in pups and youngsters. It's simply about acquiring 'dog sense'. It's not difficult to grasp but to do so requires the handler to put himself or herself in the position of the dog – undoubtedly an enlightening experience. How many times do you look in a dog's eyes and actually see it working out a situation? So try applying some dog sense and put yourself in the dog's position when a training issue presents itself.

So we have established that pups and youngsters should be seven to eight months old before any formal training starts. I believe that by this age the pup is more receptive, more able to assimilate information and instruction and there has been plenty of time to build up a good level of communication and trust in the owner. I always avoid conflict with youngsters and aim to achieve that by not allowing them get into situations where I know things may go wrong and require correction. The 'pre school' months can be the most valuable is forging bonds of mutual respect and confidence; you never get that time back with a dog so it's important not to miss the opportunity of using it to the full.

Resist any temptations to start throwing canvas puppy dummies about to see if your pup will retrieve; of course it will, that's what it's bred for. Leave all of this until there's a modicum more brain power to absorb what's going on. Resist heelwork and square-bashing and don't get hung up about sitting and staying. There will be time enough for these. Focus on achieving a pup that watches your every move, that daren't take its eyes off you in case it misses something good – a treat or a word of praise. Focus on a pup's responsiveness to you and all that you do and be generous with praise and hand contact. Once you have achieved this connection and mutual understanding everything else will naturally fall into place.

This pup is a raw, untouched and relatively naïve individual. A blank sheet of paper and you should truly value that. Everything that you do will influence the pup for the rest of its life so be ever mindful of the fact that you have total control over what goes on that blank sheet. It's essential to get it right from day one and not assume that the first eight months are just a waiting game and that everything will fall into place once training starts.

As we discussed in an earlier chapter it's very important to find out as much as you can about the sire and the dam of a pup, youngster or even adult Labrador you are interested in buying. There's a huge variation in the attitude, level of learning ability and psychological make-up within the breed. Top trainers have methods that will harness the ability of a 'hot' dog to their benefit whereas a novice would immediately find such a dog too problematic. Likewise there are dogs that are sensitive and need a totally

Creating a partnership is fundamental to getting the best out of your dog

different approach to training. They too can be problematic to the novice because while they may appear to be easier and less challenging they are, by their very nature, in need of more support. When things go wrong with a sensitive dog it can be an even harder job for the novice to overcome than with a dog that's completely the opposite.

Let's take a case in point as far as pups are concerned. Some pups are very confident and there's a tendency to assume they have a disregard for being controlled and a lack of focus. Actions are taken to quell the confidence and if applied in the wrong way by a novice they will backfire. Confident pups that have enjoyed the kind of upbringing I have discussed in this chapter should be allowed to vent their enthusiasm in their work and be praised for it. There's plenty of time to create more control out of confidence at a later stage than there is to fire-it up again if it's quashed from the start. So if you have an exuberant pup – a bit of a Jack the Lad – work with it. In the long-run, if properly nurtured, that enthusiasm will mature into drive and determination as an accomplished working gundog. All too often dogs of this type that are drilled tirelessly in their youth in some vain effort to extinguish their *joie de vivre*, will probably develop faults such as unsteadiness or whining.

While the sensitive type of pup may appear to be the easiest to train these are the ones who can easily crumble under pressure. They may appear to demonstrate a copybook response to early and basic training but later, when presented with a situation in which they are asked to show real intuition or go marginally out of their comfort zone, problems of confidence can occur. The key is not to pile on the learning with these sensitive types on the assumption that the rate of progress in the basic elements of training will be maintained. Take care to really make sure everything is well

It's important that a working Labrador is steady and responsive to all its handler's instructions

and truly learned at every stage and don't be in a hurry to move on to more testing training exercises. With sensitive types make sure you re-affirm all that is taught and when the day comes that you realise you have just asked too much and you get that look of 'I don't know what you want' or 'I am not sure I can do that' – waste no time in going back to the basics and start to build up again from the beginning of that exercise.

It might be useful here to discuss those dogs that are neither over confident nor sensitive. The perfect dog you may say, but this type presents another challenge to the trainer. These are dogs that are outwardly rather more sensitive, often tactile and appearing to need support. In training they can be exactly the opposite and show a tenacity and drive that belies their apparent innocence. The true and rather complex psychological make-up of these dogs isn't often identified by novice handlers who assume they have a saint on their hands only to find that once training starts they have a very different machine to deal with. But I have seen dogs of this type dealt with as though they were ultra-confident and in so doing the result has been disastrous. Dogs of this type are highly intelligent, very keen and usually with bags of drive – but that veneer of confidence is very thin. They are almost the equivalent of a split personality but can, if their character trait is indentified and dealt with appropriately, turn into outstanding working dogs. They need to be understood and their foibles forgiven in early training for the ultimate prize that will be delivered in adulthood. Don't push this type too hard and don't come down heavy for any early mistakes. I have seen clever dogs of this ilk develop frustrating faults because their intelligence was underestimated in early training.

With all training there is a tendency to progress to the next stage – longer retrieves, more difficult unseens, longer distance control – too quickly. While it may be boring to keep practicising the same tune over and over again it will sound all the more sweeter the longer you practice.

Keep it light, keep it bright and keep it short – those are the key elements of puppy training. Many novice owners feel under great pressure to achieve certain training goals with their pups. It's a situation that creates many of the problems encountered in the early stages so it's essential to approach each of the building blocks of learning in a way that ensures the pup is absolutely clear about what you want it to do. In many cases it's because information hasn't been given clearly that problems arise.

When observing some gundog training classes there's certainly a tendency for an over-formalised approach in some of the methods applied. The result is the dogs develop a rather mechanical style of work.

It's important that a working Labrador – no matter how or where it is asked to perform its task – is steady and responsive to all its handler's instructions. It will stop immediately when told to do so, will respond to directions and will hunt in a given area. Of course a working Labrador needs a host of other skills – to jump, to swim and to take runners in the shooting field – but basically we are trying to produce a dog that listens to what we want it to do, responds to a visual command and carries out the instruction given.

Training regimes and the schedule of training employed by some gundog clubs tends to focus too much in the initial stages on the rigid formality of precise heelwork and steadiness. While it is essential to have a Labrador that walks correctly with the handler and is steady to all temptations in the shooting field, youngsters can become very stale if a strict chronological format of training is adhered to too rigidly.

Moving through the first few months of training and leaving a few rough edges along the way isn't a problem. I like to progress steadily a

The early weeks are critical and help to develop the correct attitude, response and connection pup's elementary education giving it a degree of variety in its work providing the dog is developing rather than regressing and isn't developing faults as a consequence. It's vital to maintain the enjoyment and enthusiasm in youngsters. Trying to attain perfection at every stage dulls the dog's interest and intensifies pressure on the handler.

The pup is a blank sheet of paper and you should truly value that

# CHAPTER SIX

•

# Feeding – Getting it Right

I F LABRADORS HAVE A reputation above all things it's that they love their food and while a healthy Labrador is rarely a 'fussy feeder' it does mean they'll eat just about anything that's put in front of them. But there is a down-side to that and a lot of working Labradors aren't always fed as well as they could be in terms of the nutritional value of their diet. It's not necessarily a situation brought about through the ill intention of owners but more often through a lack of knowledge and understanding of how to feed a working gundog correctly.

Dog owners spend almost £2 billion a year feeding their dogs but within the UK market there are several large manufacturers who specialise in producing a range of feeds for working gundogs. There are others producing 'breed specific' diets – albeit primarily for pet owners but within this range there is a diet formulated solely for Labradors – but more of this later.

Working Labradors, like all working gundogs, have varying nutritional requirements depending on the time of year and their work commitments. It isn't simply a case of feeding more of a summer-time feed to a dog in winter because it's working harder. To maintain a dog in tip-top physical condition during the shooting season it's important to have a sound understanding of how you can meet its precise needs. There is now a comprehensive range of feeds on the market to help you achieve this, so it's simply a

Working Labradors
have varying nutritional
requirements
depending on the time
of year and their work
commitments

case of knowing what to feed and when to feed it. However it's important to point out that it doesn't have to be in the midst of the shooting season in the depths of December for a Labrador to need an adjustment to its diet. Any dog actively taking part in working tests in the summer or receiving regular daily training, must be receiving a diet that meets its nutritional requirements. While a working gundog in the winter needs to be in good physical condition that doesn't mean it has to be 'rib thin' – a state seen far too often and caused by dogs clearly being under-fed or not being fed the correct diet to match their energy needs.

It isn't unusual to hear some owners say they have difficulty keeping 'condition' – in other words weight – on their dogs in the shooting season. But in nearly almost every case it's simply that the dog isn't being fed enough and is certainly not being fed enough of the food he really needs in terms of its nutritional value.

While physical fitness is essential in a working gundog, expecting a dog to work throughout the shooting season when it's clearly under-weight can often have a sting in the tail in terms of health and definitely fertility in both dogs and bitches. It's essential that working gundogs are correctly fed and that their varying nutritional requirements are always met to ensure dogs remain in good health and able to lead long and active lives.

While complete diets are now the most popular method of feeding dogs it may be appropriate at this stage to consider briefly the other options. Traditionally gundogs were fed – like many other working dogs – on flesh with possibly some soaked flake maize or wholemeal biscuit added. In my youth I fed my dogs on tripe sourced from the local abattoir. It was boiled in an old wash-boiler, minced when cold and mixed with wholemeal biscuit. The dogs relished it and thrived on it. But the question that is now so often asked is why do dogs, which are carnivores, need any biscuit or carbohydrate in their diet at all? I recall the owners of a world-renowned kennel of Dalmatians whose large number of dogs were housed in a range of brick-built kennels with runs attached. The dogs were fed exclusively on bullock's heads that were split and thrown over the top of the runs every day. No cereal was fed. The dogs were always in outstanding condition.

Alas, that isn't a system of feeding many would want to follow today but similar approaches still have their devotees. Nowadays the preference for feeding raw food to dogs is known as the BARF (Bones And Raw Food) diet and for most of those who choose this method it involves feeding raw chicken – primarily chicken carcasses – as the mainstay of the dog's nutrition. In addition raw fruit and vegetables are also fed. To make it more convenient the BARF diet is also now available as deep frozen 'ready meals' but many who prefer to feed this way adhere to the simple method of feeding raw chicken carcasses or chicken wings and achieve very good results with dogs that look fit and healthy.

While boiling tripe in a wash-boiler isn't everyone's idea of having a good time there are still those who prefer to feed their dogs on a traditional diet of 'meat and biscuits'. Frozen tripe and a range of other frozen meats are readily available and remain a popular option. The debate as to whether the precise nutritional needs of working dogs can be met with simplified diets such as the BARF diet or one based on meat and cereal will certainly continue, but for owners deliberating over how best to feed their dog I would urge all options to be considered.

Despite all the advertising and advice that is available there is still a great deal of confusion about feeding dogs – and particularly pups and young dogs during their critical growing stages. How much to feed, what to feed and when to feed are all questions to which any enquiring owner can find a vast range of answers. However there's no doubt that the nutrition a

There are dog foods covering a wide range of protein levels and ingredients

puppy receives during its first few weeks of life has a significant impact on its growth, development and ultimately lifetime health.

The dog food industry has made massive strides over the last 30 years. As a young man I learned much by working with a leading breeder of English Springers who ran a large kennels. Complete diet feeding was still in its infancy but the owner of the kennel – who was also experienced with other livestock – formulated a cereal-based ration which was mixed by a local feed mill and fed with boiled, minced tripe cooked at the kennels. This cereal/tripe mix was fed to everything from weaned pups to adults. Pups were weaned on to minced tripe and then soon moved on to the cereal/tripe mix. No one ever questioned the protein content of the diet – the pups, youngsters and dogs all thrived in this very successful kennel where the dogs were always in outstanding physical condition.

So where does that leave us when we are faced with the seemingly ever increasing array of complete-diet dog foods? There are dog foods covering a wide range of protein levels – formulated to meet the needs of dogs at certain stages of their development, relevant to their activity levels, to their breed and also for lactating bitches. There are dog foods that are flaked and others that are extruded and covering a broad price range. No wonder there is so much confusion.

Striking a balance between a food you feel is most suited to your dog and to your pocket usually underpins the final decision. Cheap foods should be avoided. Raw ingredient prices – both the cereal and protein content of all animal feeds – are steadily rising and are likely to continue to do so which means cheap dog foods have to be made with cheap ingredients and that has an adverse effect on the standard of nutrition they can provide. But at the other end of the spectrum there are extremely expensive feeds – some five times more costly than the lower-priced complete diets – something which continues to prompt questions from new owners. Cheap feeds may appear to have an analysis of their ingredients that looks extremely similar to that which appears on the side of the bag of a food five times the price, but the source of the ingredients in the cheap food will be of lower quality – and of less value nutritionally.

It's always worth remembering that protein can be obtained from a wide variety of sources – even leather boot laces and green nettles contain protein! While the protein content of a complete diet is very important, it's essential to select a brand you feel is using a high quality and consistent source of protein. While the superior feeds use meat meal to provide protein, it's not unusual for some manufacturers of the lower-grade feeds to use soya meal, maize gluten or potato protein. These will provide sources of protein but they aren't the best and can certainly create health issues for some dogs.

The fat content of dog foods is another constituent of the formulation that can cause confusion. There is a school of thought that believes the fat level of a complete diet dog food should be a prime consideration when evaluating the formulation and analysis. Fat is undoubtedly an important inclusion but again it depends on the source of the fat. Fat levels range from around 8% to 14% but cheap feeds are more likely to look for lower-cost fat sources which can contain high levels of saturated fats.

Before we look more closely at the types of feeds on the market and a dog's varying requirements as it progresses through life, let's first try to ensure the ingredients in your dog's food are of a high enough standard. As mentioned earlier, ingredient prices are rising so when the cost of a particular brand of dog food appears to stay the same you may think the manufacturer is simply trying not to pass price rises on to its customers. In truth it's more likely that price increases have been avoided because ingredient quality has been sacrificed in favour of avoiding a retail price rise. You don't have to go far to talk to a gundog owner to hear tales of how a dog was on the same food and doing well when suddenly it either started to refuse it or suffered some sort of stomach upset. The likelihood is that there was an

It's essential to maintain a dog in tip-top physical condition during the shooting season (*Photo: Sharon Rogers*)

ingredient change – nothing that would be noticeable as such on the list of ingredients that have, by law, to be written on the side of the bag, but certainly the 'quality' and even the source of an ingredient may have been changed.

Rather than opt for a manufacturer who produces only one formulation of dog food, it's better to select a company marketing a range of feeds. The range will probably include a high protein puppy food, possibly a junior food or a mix that is recommended as the next stage on from puppyhood (post six-months), as well as a lower-protein (18%) diet for dogs when not working. There may even be a higher protein mix for dogs with a high energy requirement (23–24%) and an even higher protein mix (29%) for pregnant and lactating bitches. This type of manufacturer's range presents a comprehensive selection of feeds to choose from and enables owners to remain with one manufacturer for all their dog's requirements.

Some manufacturers are now producing feeds for specific breeds but some designed for Labradors do appear to have a rather high protein content (26%) when one considers they have primarily been formulated for the 'pet' owner. Dogs working hard in the shooting season should be able to thrive off an established brand offering a complete diet of 23% protein and 10% fat if fed at the correct rate to meet the dog's needs. I use the Skinner's range of feeds to provide formulations to suit all stages of rearing as well as the varying needs of adult dogs in terms of their level of work or the time of year.

One of the biggest issues many new owners face when trying to select a dog food is the lack of advice available at point of sale. Pet shops and country stores sell a wide range of foods but are rarely able to give independent advice. So when deciding on what feed to use try to do as much research as possible and then make direct contact with a manufacturer to answer your questions. Game Fairs and country sports gatherings are often attended by representatives of the leading gundog food manufacturers who are always ready to provide all the practical information you need.

In the past it was very uncommon for dogs to suffer dietary problems and intolerances and yet now it seems as rife in dogs as it is in humans. In so many cases these health issues are caused by incorrect feeding – either because of the feed that's used or the regime of feeding. Selecting a high quality food produced by a responsible and established company with a strong connection with working gundogs and adopting a feed regime that enables a dog to eat and digest it's food correctly, will produce a healthier and more responsive working gundog.

## Wet, dry, ad-lib

Labradors are greedy feeders by and large so feeding any complete diet in its dry state is not only dangerous for the dog but is a totally alien way of consuming feed. As a flesh eating carnivore, a dog would never eat totally dry food. Many owners do feed their dogs with un-moistened food but if you have ever watched a Labrador gulp down a bowl of dry food and then imagine what it feels like to have eaten a plate of dry cream crackers in record time, you get some idea of how that feels for the dog. Dogs that 'bolt' their food are not uncommon in the Labrador breed; it's a trait that I have occasionally had to deal with in the past even when feeding moistened food. Some dogs that eat by simply trying to gulp and swallow large mouthfuls of dry food can end up with abrasions to the oesophagus. These problems can make it so painful that the dog refuses to eat or eats and then vomits it back.

After 40 years of experience I would always advise feeding complete feeds moistened with water – just 'off the boil' – to create a palatable, but definitely not sloppy, consistency.

Ad-lib feeding – where food is available to dogs all day long – isn't an option for adult Labradors. I wouldn't advise this method even be attempted. I have seen litters of pups where a tray or hopper of food has provided round-the-clock availability but again, it's not something I would recommend.

## How I feed at Fenway

Everyone has their own way of feeding dogs but in my Fenway kennels I believe good nutrition is fundamental to correct dog management – not only to maintain a dog's correct physical condition but also in the part it plays in a dog's attitude to its life and work and to its long term well-being. That may appear to be taking a rather convoluted overview of feeding dogs – which to many people is simply a case of putting something in a bowl and leaving the rest to the dog – but it's one to which I adhere very closely.

As I have already discussed, food is undoubtedly a big part of any Labrador's life so it's important that feeding takes place at the same time every day – wherever possible. Routine is the key to managing working dogs and feeding time is an important part of that. In the Fenway kennels all the adult dogs are fed twice a day – a small meal in the morning at around 7am and a main meal in the evening at around 5pm.

The 'kennel kitchen' is very much that and is stocked with a range of Skinner's foods. No single diet (in terms of protein content) is fed to the same dog all the time or in the same quantities all the time. A range of factors will influence what's fed to each dog at each feeding time and how much is fed.

This is not a complicated system and it means that the dogs are not over-fed or underfed. It is impossible to expect a dog to hold the right amount of body condition and be healthy if it receives the same food in the same quantity every day.

I maintain a constant awareness of the body condition of every dog while out at exercise or training. It only takes a glance but it's sufficient to indicate how the dog is looking physically. That decision forms the basis of how the dog is fed on that particular day.

Physical fitness has a lot to do with a dog's diet
*(Photo: Sharon Rogers)*

The factors I take into account are based on how much work the dog is doing – either in training, competition or in the shooting field. I would also consider the weather particularly if it's a cold spell and dogs are clearly burning up more energy than they would be in warmer conditions. I consider the age of the dog – growing pups up to six-months old will be on three feeds a day – and we are also very mindful of the needs of individuals and any senior dogs. Every dog is different in the way it assimilates food and even individuals change as they get older.

So when the kettle is switched on in the kennel kitchen at Fenway at each end of the day a mental note has been taken about the body condition of each dog as well as all the other prevailing circumstances. But that doesn't automatically mean the quantity to be fed to each dog has been decided. The Skinner's range of dog foods provides a high level of flexibility. Out of the working season – late spring and summer – I feed predominantly an 18% protein 'maintenance' diet. At this time of year this feed provides a good basic diet and if a dog needs a high volume of food we simply increase the amount being fed.

When dogs are more active during the shooting season – or if I feel a dog during the summer has been training hard – I feed a 23% protein feed. The Skinner's range enables me to feed a variety of diets from within the range and to 'mix and match' so a dog can be moved 'up' from an 18% to a 23% for a couple of days or just for alternate feeds if I feel that's what's needed – and I can do it without risk of any dietary stomach upsets.

The 18% and 23% protein diets are my two basic rations and by feeding in this flexible way I can maintain dogs in good physical condition and avoid sudden weight gain or weight loss. Monitoring the condition of dogs daily is a critical part of good canine nutrition – and no more so than in working dogs.

I also use the Skinner's Muesli mix (20%) protein. This is a very useful feed especially on days when a dog has been working in cold or wet conditions and needs something to really sit on its stomach. If I fed Muesli to

Working Labradors expend a great deal of energy on a shoot day
(Photo: Anne Taylor)

a dog in the evening after a hard day's work I'd give a higher protein feed the following morning – probably 23%. But I always have a 27% protein feed on hand to give a 'shot' of energy to the hardest workers.

The 27% protein feed is used primarily for pregnant bitches once pregnancy is confirmed and before the quality of the diet increases to a 30% protein diet just prior to whelping – and for the first few weeks after the birth to ensure the bitch is lactating at her optimum level.

If a stud dog is being worked hard in the shooting season and also has stud duties I'd be mindful of making sure he was on a higher protein-based diet for some of his feeds. A rising plane of nutrition is fundamental to improving fertility in all livestock. Any animal whose body reserves are under pressure when expected to breed will suffer a downturn in fertility as the body's natural reaction for survival is not to reproduce. Similarly, if I have one of my own bitches to mate I'd automatically put her on to a rising plane of nutrition – a higher protein diet – once she came into season and continue that for two weeks after the mating to improve the levels of embryo implantation.

My dogs are always fed individually. This is very important. All dogs eat at different speeds. You may think that every Labrador gulps down its food but that's not the case.

The only supplement used at Fenway is Dorwest 'Keepers Mix' which is a herbal powder based on seaweed and nettles and is a product we've used for many years. It's an excellent supplement for general good health, excellent for coats and skin – and I believe boosts fertility.

While the mature dogs are fed twice a day, younger dogs are fed according to their age. Pups are fed Skinner's Puppy Food from three weeks old. This is liquidised initially before progressing to feeding it very well-soaked with water off the boil. I like to have baby pups on four meals a day as soon as possible. Goat's milk is also used – usually given as a drink after feeding. Pups stay on four meals until about 12 weeks and while it's important not to over-feed pups it's also dangerous to suddenly start to cut back on food if pups are putting on too much weight. Regular feeding is the key to sustained growth and development. I prefer to marginally reduce the amount being fed rather than suddenly cut out a meal at this stage of growth.

Pups remain on the 26% Skinner's Puppy Food until six months old – and start receiving their daily Keepers Mix from about 12 weeks old. Pups are fed morning, lunch, late afternoon and again in late evening. By six months I start to make a gradual change to the diet and introduce a 23% protein feed so that by the time pups are just over six month old they are on two meals a day of the 23% protein diet.

## Adopt the correct feeding regime

Complete diets are now the most popular method of feeding working gundogs but it's important to get the best results by selecting a food you are confident will sustain your dog's health and performance. All animal food manufacturers have a legal requirement to disclose the formulation of ingredients being used in each product and while that has been a great boon to all who feed any form of livestock it's still important to be satisfied with the quality of the feed.

If you arm yourself with as much information as possible about the precise nutritional value of various foods on the market you will be able to make a considered choice.

The aim should be to match your dog's dietary needs to maintain physical condition, match the work load and take account of any other environmental influences that may have an impact.

No task is too great for a well-fed and healthy working Labrador

There has been considerable debate about the level of protein fed to young dogs and pups. In the past young dogs weren't fed such 'high octane' feeds and those who now question this practice do so in the belief that it increases the rate of development and in consequence can pre-dispose young dogs to joint problems, particularly in the elbow.

The alternative is to feed a lower protein diet, say from three months old, but critics say this can have an adverse effect on the pup's nutritional needs at a critical stage in its physical development.

In my experience I believe it's appropriate and beneficial to maintain the protein level in the feed at 24–26% up to the three-month stage and then to switch to a slightly lower protein puppy food.

## When to feed

Dogs kept as individuals, whether kennelled or kept in the house, are clearly going to have a different life-style to those kept as part of a larger group. It's very likely that many owners will be away from their dogs for part of the day and that in itself creates a situation that should be taken into account when adopting an appropriate feeding regime that suits you and one that is of most benefit to the dog.

I have already mentioned routine and it's something that is even more important to single dog owners – particularly at feeding time. The level of intelligence that an owner taps into with his working Labrador doesn't switch 'on and off' as training sessions or days in the field start and end. The instruction that you impart during training and the responses you expect are equally fine-tuned to all the other occurrences in the dog's day.

While training and working a dog is the real 'buzz' of owning a working Labrador, your dog maintains an equally acute awareness of other things, many of which you may perceive as being rather mundane – such as feeding time.

Feeding at different times in the morning or evening; feeding in different locations in the house, even different people being given the job of actually doing the feeding, can all 'jar' on the intelligent routine of a working dog. That may seem far fetched but it is true. The stability and routine you are encouraged to impart to the dog when training or out shooting should be mirrored in the routine of its 'domestic' life. So in the morning the dog should be allowed out to relieve himself and if then taken for more vigorous exercise he should not be fed before that takes place and not immediately after. Dogs should be allowed to settle before feeding and then always allowed to sleep afterwards. In its natural state a dog would kill to eat, consume the prey and then sleep to digest the meal. Dogs always, if allowed to, switch into a calmer, quieter state after feeding if given the opportunity.

In the evening, if the dog has been left alone for some time, it's not advisable to suddenly give the dog vigorous exercise – because you feel he has been cooped up all day – and then put a bowl full of food in front of it. Better to let the dog out to relieve itself and if possible have an area where the dog can just stretch and exercise for a short period before being fed. After feeding allow for the sleep period and only after at least one hour, when the meal has settled, should you consider other exercise or training.

All in a day's work!
*(Photo: Frank Toti)*

Many new starters to gundog training experience difficulties with young dogs at evening classes or when summer training undertaken at the end of the day when the owner has been at work. This is often associated with the dog's mental and physical state – and a lot to do with the feeding regime. So make sure the dog is rested after being fed and before training starts, or if necessary delay feeding until after the training session.

•

# CHAPTER SEVEN

# Nurturing Working Ability

RAINING A WORKING Labrador is well within the capabilities of most people but it has to be a two-way process and not approached purely with the intention of achieving 'blind' obedience through the application of a rigid set of training methods.

Some may be surprised by that ethos but while you, as the owner and handler of the dog, have to be in control and impart your instructions to ensure the dog can do its job as effectively as possible, to achieve a sustainable and successful working partnership, there has to be mutual respect on both sides.

Nevertheless it's essential to give some thought to precisely where you are starting from in terms of your experience and not to lose sight of exactly what you are aspiring to achieve.

Everything in life has an ultimate target and while attaining a level of excellence is the driving force, for the most part we have to be realistic and set ourselves achievable goals. As we have discussed previously, the working ability of Labradors has, as its benchmark, the world of field trials where skilled handlers compete with highly trained dogs and are judged on their performance over shot game. While dogs that compete at the top level demonstrate an exceptionally high standard of work, the challenge for most owners of working Labradors is how to train their dogs in a way – and to a standard – that's achievable.

Field trials remain an intensely competitive interest for those involved and they are still regarded as the 'university' from which the best dogs emerge with their appropriate Field Trial Champion title in recognition of their achievements.

The title represents a set of credentials the world of working Labradors has come to recognise as the approved 'level of excellence' and one that continues to be revered.

The aim for most novices is to produce a sensible, accomplished and responsive working gundog

Dogs that have earned the title of Field Trial Champion have wide appeal – among puppy buyers looking for a pup from a well-bred litter and among those selecting a sire for a bitch.

But without taking any of the kudos away from these title holders, do we need to ask the question: 'Are the methods used to hone the skills of competitive field trial dogs truly applicable to the average owner intending to train a working Labrador?' While it is essential to have a benchmark of skills upon which all retriever training must be based, many dogs in the hands of novice owners are well below the potential standard of those that will go on to win open stake awards, even though they can effectively fulfil their role as working Labradors. While we mustn't lower our expectations of a working Labrador's ability as a shooting dog or as a member of a picking-up team, it's clear that the difficulties many newcomers encounter when training young dogs are the result of some of the training methods they are advised to use – methods that have evolved with field trials as the primary aim.

As the type of dog and the style of work needed to win field trials has changed over the last 50 years, so have the training methods used. We seem to have fallen into a training doctrine that applies more pressure to young dogs – and has greater expectations at a much younger age – than many novice trainers can cope with.

The aim for most novices is to produce a sensible, accomplished and responsive working gundog and to do that I believe we need to look at a less pressured approach to training. Greater emphasis is needed to forge and nurture a stronger and fundamental 'connection' between dog and handler from the very earliest stages and then to introduce and develop skills and ability within the partnership.

The word 'connection' is the very essence of training any dog. Developing this level of rapport creates a working relationship where no challenges are too great.

## Discipline – why and to what end?

There are widely varying levels of discipline meted out to all dogs being trained for all sorts of jobs, but applying severe chastisement as a means of engendering fear in the dog as the basis for achieving obedience, isn't an approach I agree with and is one that many novice trainers don't want to use. *The 'fear-based fast-track' attitude to training is inappropriate and unacceptable* for most of today's novice trainers.

Gundog training can certainly be challenging and frustrating as well as hugely satisfying, but training methods need to start looking more precisely at the role of the end product – and for the most part that end product is a shooting dog or a picking-up dog.

There's no doubt that to *get the best from a dog he has to work with you and not for you.* There has to be a solid partnership from the start. In so many cases training issues arise because there is no real bond between the dog and the owner. Suddenly the relationship becomes driven by pressure to learn and the owner is regarded more as a teacher and oppressor by the dog, rather than a dependable partner.

Applying physical discipline – and applying it more severely as a means of driving home a message even harder – isn't something I feel has any worthwhile part in creating that relationship. Harsh, physical discipline may often appear to have corrected one problem in the short-term, but so often another problem crops up later as a consequence. Coping with this ripple effect of training problems is far from an ideal situation for a novice trainer to cope with; it only serves to widen the rift between dog and handler.

On a shooting day I noticed a rather nice young black dog with someone I had never seen before. The dog had a genuine attitude to his work, although he was clearly a little sensitive at times which made him over-cautious and often miss the mark of a bird's fall. But he was a very honest dog when he was focussed. His handler was clearly a novice and the partnership was lacking some confidence. I wasn't the only person to notice the dog so it was interesting to hear something about him when two of us approached the owner. Seemingly the dog had been a very keen youngster and the handler was inexperienced. He took the dog to a well-known trainer, the dog ran in at the first retrieve and the owner admitted that the corrective treatment given to the dog as a consequence of his misdemeanour disturbed him. The dog hadn't run in since but the owner admitted he was now a very different dog and had become hesitant and less confident in his attitude to work. What a shame that a dog with potential – albeit with an issue to correct – had had the life knocked out of him when his keenness could so easily have been dealt with in a more positive way.

So for those who need a well-trained Labrador as a shooting dog, to join a picking-up team or even to take a tilt at a few working tests, training methods must be based initially on developing a close 'connection' of mutual trust between dog and handler and not one that's fear-based and requires excessive shouting, lead jerking and shaking.

Many will have heard of Edward Martin who founded the Sealpin kennels in the Scottish Borders. Edward's training methods are exemplary but while he is totally fair and positive in all he achieves with his dogs, everything is based on the premise 'on my terms'. That, in no way, infers any kind of severe training. It simply means 'we're a partnership but I call the tune – fairly but always'. And that is such an important part of the relationship we must create with all dogs in training.

Establishing 'connection' in no way undermines the way the dog perceives its handler in terms of leadership. How you respond when the relationship is tested or when mistakes occur will directly affect how quickly he learns.

A dog's hunting skills are acute *(Photo: Sharon Rogers)*

Come down heavily on a dog in that situation and you immediately undermine trust between you rather than strengthen it. A dog learns respect and is more committed to his work if you take a responsible attitude when things go wrong. Tone of voice is absolutely crucial and later we'll look more closely at how this is applied effectively to express displeasure.

*Dogs don't deliberately do things wrong based on a decision on their part to disobey you.* They do what they do because they don't know any better at the time. Yes, some dogs are faster learners than others and some are inherently cleverer than others. But that doesn't mean that applying correction will sort out an error of a slow learner and speed up the learning process or even make the dim dog any brighter!

There's no doubt that some dogs are much easier to train than others and when you see virtually novice handlers suddenly emerge with great success on to the field trial scene it's either because they are naturally good handlers and have an outstanding relationship with their dog or they have been fortunate in having a dog that has been very easily trained.

Applying pain to the dog as a means of correction and with the intention that he will learn from the experience is something I cannot understand or see the value of. Does the dog understand that undergoing pain is directly linked to an action just committed? And even if it did have the ability to reason in that way, does suffering the pain enable it to understand that if it does the same action again it will once again suffer the punishment?

I know there will be many who say they effectively make use of harsh correction in their training methods and see no adverse impact on their dogs, but that still doesn't vindicate their actions in my view. Because of their experience, and more often because they will only work with dogs able to cope with that sort of training, they are able to achieve some sort of result. But for the novice the outcome is all too often less positive.

Combining good game sense, biddability and a level of speed and agility that can be effectively controlled almost at the push of a button are the impressive traits that form the basis of the most exciting displays of Labrador work in field trials. Most dogs have all those skills, but in varying degrees of ability; the challenge as a trainer is having the skill to upgrade the negatives and harness the positives. Two negatives never make a positive, so administering negative methods to try to improve an existing negativity is a road to nowhere.

## Building confidence

I never intentionally put a young dog in a situation where he will probably fail. If the building blocks of training are stacked carefully one on top of the other, stage by careful stage, they shouldn't come tumbling down. If they do, the best way forward is to start from the bottom and build them up again by taking the dog back to the basics of what he was being taught and re-visit the original principles because it's clear he's not fully grasped what's wanted. Again we come back to patience and time – they yield the biggest payback.

If the building blocks of training are stacked carefully, stage by stage, they shouldn't come tumbling down

## The stop

One of the most important things any working gundog must learn is how to respond to the stop whistle. If you are able to stop your dog at distance – long or short – and hold the dog in that position you can immediately take control of any situation.

As I have already mentioned, I will often 'pip' a pup up to me and give a hand signal to sit and a longer 'pip' – all undertaken very informally and probably from about three or four months old depending on the pup. Most pups will respond to this almost unknowingly and yet you are laying the foundations of teaching the 'stop'.

As time progresses – and again depending on the pup – I will give a 'pip' on the whistle when the pup is perhaps about 10 yards or so away from me. Usually the pup will stop and look and possibly think about coming towards me but with the hand held high in giving the sit command (although at this stage it is acting rather more as a halt signal) I may give another single 'pip' and with purposeful body language and probably a step forward I can almost 'hold' the pup in the stop position from a distance. It's a case of what the pup hears and the visual messages you are sending physically. No shouting, no scare tactics. You have presented the pup with a set of audible and visual commands and he has to learn to read those signals. If it isn't learnt immediately just repeat but perhaps at a shorter distance. If the pup does sit and stay as the command requested, I then walk over to the pup and praise it, although always remembering to maintain my positive body posture to re-affirm my control of the situation.

In a situation where a youngster decides not to respond to the stop whistle firstly make sure you have the dog's attention and achieve that by blowing repeatedly on the whistle. Then walk towards the dog with your right hand held high, palm facing towards the dog. I can assure you that at some point he will stop. When he does you must walk towards the dog and praise him. If given harsh treatment he won't associate it with not stopping at the outset, but now he has stopped and praise is due. You have avoided conflict and ended on a positive note. Now it's you who should get cross (inwardly) with yourself for allowing that to happen and you need to go back to re-affirming the exercise in a confined area. When you do progress to a more open space don't go back to where it went wrong the first time and try to apply the exercise over a reduced distance. You as the

One of the most important things any working gundog must learn is how to respond to the stop whistle

handler need to learn from what went wrong, not just the dog, and yet we always assume that because the dog made an error it is all his fault – and that's not fair or good dog training. Just think how you would deal with a child that was learning to swim; you wouldn't expect the child to try out quickly his skills in deep water and get annoyed if the child started to drown!

## Staying in the comfort zone

*Familiarity doesn't breed contempt in working gundogs – it should be used as an important aid to training.*

All working gundogs have an inherent ability to do the job they were bred for. Some are better than others but there are those that have plenty of talent but lack the confidence to apply it consistently. To help build confidence I like to repeat the same lesson to the same dog in the same area.

Yes, the dog does soon learn what's wanted and for me that's absolutely what I want to happen. I do not want to challenge the dog at this stage or make him feel uneasy and unconfident. I want to build on his ability and self-belief and if that can be achieved by the fact that he almost knows what's going to happen and where the dummy will be thrown then all well and good. It's all compounding his skills, boosting his confidence and helping him succeed.

Even when I move on to elementary work on blind (unseen) retrieves I place dummies in the same place repeatedly. I don't see this as ineffective and giving the dog an advantage, I see it as confirming in the dog's mind that whenever I point him and send him in a certain direction he finds what he has been sent for. With each unseen retrieve, no matter how basic, he is believing in me more and more, so that he will reach a point where the location and the distance are immaterial – the fact that he is sent away from me and follows the direction in which he has been sent and he gets a result is what I am aiming for. So never feel that the same location for training is becoming too familiar to the young dog in the early stages; there's always plenty of time and plenty of situations when he will be out of his comfort zone but will hopefully have developed the confidence to deal with that because he has total trust in you and what you are asking him to do.

Visual and vocal commands are essential in early training on the stop whistle

Dogs don't gain in self-confidence or experience more rapidly by taking them to the edge of their ability purely as a means of letting them get it wrong and giving the handler the opportunity to apply corrective pressure. The best advice is not to put young dogs into situations where there is a good chance they will fail. Repetitive though it may be, it's far better to reinforce the learning process at each stage in a situation where you have control and the dog knows you have control.

## Body talk

But all this is about patience – and so much can be communicated by means other than voice. Dogs don't speak; they don't comprehend what we say as such but operate by linking together an association of the sound of the command and the action they have been taught to perform. Let's put voice commands aside for a moment and look at how dogs communicate with themselves. They rely solely on their senses. Smell is the primary canine sense and communication by sight comes second. How dogs respond to one another is very much about body language and yet not enough use is made of this during training. When the wrong posture and deportment is adopted by the handler when working with the dog it sends many conflicting signals – some of negativity, some of anger, some of no confidence and often no leadership. It creates insecurity.

When training a dog you are the lynch pin. The conduit that links the dog and the command. Your stance, your hand movements, the positive or negative energy that transmits to the dog will have a significant impact on how the dog performs. How the dog leaves you for a retrieve, how it sees you when it looks back asking for a handling instruction or encouragement and how it assesses your demeanour when it returns. With a pup or a young dog I believe body language – the way commands are given physically through the body, arms and hands and even the look on the face of the handler – are absolutely crucial to the end result.

## Don't get hung up on the negatives

All dogs can excel at certain things but have weaknesses in others. Novice trainers who have a dog with real ability in some quarters but less in others can quickly become paranoid about the negatives – the secret is not to get too hung up about it because more often than not the problems are never as insurmountable as you imagine.

A preoccupation by the handler with a specific training problem can undermine the positive aspects of the progress being made in other areas and weaken the 'connection' between dog and handler.

It's easy for displeasure and frustration to permeate across the entire relationship and trigger doubt and insecurity in the dog's mind – even when he's undertaking part of his work that he's normally good at. How many times have we heard people comment that they have been trying to correct one fault only to find that another has crept in. And it's all because confidence has been tested and weakened as a consequence.

It's important that we train gundogs in a way that most people can adopt and apply and subsequently achieve the desired end result – a dog that suits the owner's purpose. Many people training their first dog end up trying to follow a training strategy they can't apply effectively and even if they can, it's not one that will ultimately produce for them the dog they want.

A typical case in point concerns a man who contacted me about a fully-trained dog he had bought. He'd paid a lot of money for the dog and both he, and others, were impressed with its ability. The dog was something of a machine; well trained and on the button but not a dog that gave much of himself to his new owner. A dog with a job but not much else going for him. So impressed was one fellow Gun on the shoot that he asked to use the dog at stud. The owner agreed and took a pup in lieu of the stud fee. But then he encountered a problem. The dog refused to leave bitches – any bitches – alone. So bad did this lustful dog become that the owner had to start leaving him at home on shoot days. The owner asked me why it had happened and what he should do – having tried all ways to dissuade the dog from his amorous antics. I admitted that with an older dog like this he was facing an uphill struggle; given time and effort I believe he would be able to correct the problem but the essence of the dog's failure to respond to his owner's repeated efforts is largely due to the fact that they don't actually have any real relationship as dog and owner – no connection. The dog is a machine that has come across a situation that it has never come across before and the lack of any real understanding between the two of them has resulted in this problem of unwanted behaviour.

It's important to remember that a dog, any dog, doesn't have the ability – nor I believe the desire – to make a conscious decision to be difficult. For all those who have endured a frustrating training session or been shooting or picking up or in a test or a trial when a dog has done something wholly unacceptable, that may be difficult to accept – but it's true. A dog failing to carry out a command or taking it upon itself to do something that it shouldn't is only carrying out that action because it doesn't know any better at that moment. Now you may say that is also wrong

because when a dog has been taught to do something correctly, the fact that it suddenly does the opposite is pure defiance. Incorrect again. The reason the dog exhibited that 'defiance' could probably be attributed to a weakness in his training – but is more likely to have been simply 'dog error'. Let's not forget these are dogs and remember that even humans aren't infallible.

Whatever it takes to do the job – well-trained working dogs are totally focussed on finding and retrieving game *(Photo: Peter Bates)*

# CHAPTER EIGHT

·

# Managing the Adult Labrador

THERE CAN BE FEW BREEDS as undemanding as the adult Labrador. While that should in no way assume that caring for a Labrador during its adult life means an owner can be any less committed than with any other breed, I often feel that once a Labrador has passed the exuberance of puppyhood and is through the stage of possibly being a headstrong youngster, its real needs can easily get over-looked. Quite often a case of 'job done.'

Labradors kept as working gundogs will either be kennelled outside or live in the house with the family. So let's look at how to get the best from both those regimes of management in terms of what's best for the dog and for you as the owner.

## Kennel life

As we have discussed in an earlier chapter it's important to buy the right type of kennel from the outset and while a young pup may look somewhat lost in a kennel designed for an adult dog, that pup will be adult size and have adult housing needs within less than 12 months from the day he arrives.

Purpose-built kennels are now widely available – some are good and some are less so. Unfortunately a Labrador will learn to survive in a small space but that should be no excuse to limit the size of the dog's accommo-dation. But before we address how much area a Labrador really needs to provide a healthy environment to meet its welfare needs, let's first consider what a kennel actually has to provide.

Protection from the elements is a primary function of the adult dog's kennel but it must also provide a degree of comfort. A working Labrador kept outside is even more deserving of a decent standard of welfare than a Labrador kept as a house pet. So a good standard of kennelling is essential to provide a place in which the dog can live comfortably and in an environ-ment appropriate for his role in life. Anything that can be done, in terms of kennel design to ensure the dog remains in the best mental and physical state during its adult life, should be a priority consideration. And remem-ber that your pup will quickly demand accommodation as befits an adult working gundog.

Gundogs kennelled outside must have a healthy environment to meet all aspects of their welfare

There are now many manufacturers of kennels and kennel systems using a variety of materials – from timber to plastic. But in selecting a kennel it's important to look at the quality of the materials used to ensure they can provide durability, comfort and security as well as a means of containment.

Most Labradors as young dogs love to chew wood and while good quality timber kennels provide the best type of adult accommodation, consideration must be given to damage caused by chewing. Anti-chew strips can be fitted and anti-chew spray can be effective.

The quality of the timber and its treatment by the manufacturer is important. Thin, untreated timber won't endure the wear and tear of the fixtures and fittings inside and more importantly won't provide the dog with the protection it needs. A strong and sturdy construction is essential to house an adult Labrador and the most well-known manufacturers provide this. Depending on the actual siting of the kennel – in terms of wind and weather – it's worth having all timber surfaces lined internally to provide additional insulation. This must definitely be undertaken for the sleeping area the dog uses at the rear of the kennel. And it's important to make sure the sleeping area is raised well above the floor to prevent cold and damp striking upwards.

It's important to have an awareness of what your dog will actually be doing during the periods he is left alone in his kennel. Will he sleep for most of the time? Will he sit in his run and longingly wait for your return or will he amuse himself with anything you can provide to 'enrich' his kennel environment? Always be mindful of the fact that this is an intelligent working gundog with an active brain and his day to day kennel environment needs to take account of that.

We shouldn't assume that a working gundog must never be given anything to 'play' with in its kennel for fear of it having an adverse effect on its attitude to work or running the risk of creating a hard-mouthed dog or one that doesn't handle game correctly during a retrieve. I've never found this to be the case if the correct items are provided in the kennel for mental stimulus. Hard, tough, non-chewable items will stimulate but will not trigger bad habits.

To return to the question of what dogs actually do when their owners are away and I have to say that most – especially after exercise and food – will sleep for long periods. However I don't think that is sufficient reason to

A high standard of kennel accommodation helps maintain good health in mature dogs

severely limit the area a dog has for exercise within the kennel system they live in, but it does mean more focus should be given to the sleeping area. This part of the kennel needs to provide the dog with a warm, dry area that affords total protection from the weather. Many wooden kennel designs have a 'box' area at the back of the kennel with a pop-hole entrance. The idea being that the dog can either sleep inside the box or on top of the box. Alternatively there are designs that provide a floor to roof area at the rear of the kennel that acts as a sleeping section, usually accessed through a pop-hole by the dog and with a full-sized hinged door to enable access for cleaning. This design is useful in that it means that, providing there is adequate ventilation, the dog can be 'sectioned off' into this area at night and so keeping him away from the elements. This system also means the dog doesn't start barking if he gets disturbed by cats or owls calling in the night, although some owners prefer their dogs to be aware of night-time activity as a means of a security alert.

Within the sleeping area you will have various bedding options but as discussed earlier there is nothing to beat a good quality plastic dog bed of generous size and bedded appropriately.

Labradors do like to curl up and the curvature of the plastic bed provides them with added protection from draughts. Inside the bed you can be as imaginative as you like but much depends on the dog. Most of our adult dogs have the 'Vetbed' type fleece bedding which is widely available. If pups like to chew their bedding I switch them on to deep beds of soft wood shavings. Pieces of old carpet, old blankets and clothes aren't recommend – they aren't warm enough and can't be kept clean. The security of your dog and how you can do your best to make sure the kennel system provides him with a degree of safety will be discussed later in this chapter.

Make sure the area of the kennel building that covers the sleeping section is well felted or weather-proofed with other material and that any rain that runs off the roof isn't going to run directly into the kennel's run area and create constant puddles. Many 'complete' one-dog kennels are split into the sleeping area at the rear and the run area at the front. The run area, in my opinion, is often too small for an adult Labrador unless dogs are receiving ample exercise or work to compensate. But where an adult Labrador is expected to spend a considerable amount of its time in a small space I would advise looking at a compromise that most manufacturers can easily comply with.

Either request a larger run area or consider buying a timber building that provides somewhere for the dog to sleep and using the widely available galvanised mesh kennel-run sections to construct a larger exercise area. Thought needs to be given to the ground cover of the run area which clearly needs to provide the dog with a hard surface and one that's easily cleaned. Concrete is the preferred choice, sloping appropriately to take all water away from the area used by the dog. Paving flags are another option but gravel is not recommended – it's impossible to keep properly clean and some dogs do crunch gravel in fits of boredom often with dire consequences.

In 30 years we have only ever had one dog that was able to scale a six-feet high kennel run from a standing start! That height is usually good enough to contain even the most active Labrador. The run area can be covered but the decision will clearly depend on the size. Individual timber kennels and runs usually come with the option to be covered and it's certainly worth considering.

Providing electricity in the kennel is a big asset to winter management but all wiring and switches must be out of reach of the dog and suitably protected. Being able to light the kennel will make caring for the dog in winter much easier and it will enable additional heating to be provided if necessary. Considering the short days of winter it's worth thinking about using a timer to switch on the kennel light if you are still away from home when darkness falls. Power in the kennels will also enable you to provide some radio 'background noise' which we have always used in our kennel buildings and which has a very beneficial effect on pups and undoubtedly breaks the monotony of kennel life for mature dogs.

Security is now an issue every gundog owner must be acutely aware of and clearly any dog left unattended is going to be at risk. Making sure the kennel is of robust construction will help you to attach latches and gate closures that will ensure the dog will not break out of its own accord and will go some way to providing a secure environment. But determined thieves will not be deterred by padlocks, although making theft as difficult as possible by using the very strongest and most expensive may go some way to making access more difficult – even if they simply buy a few minutes of extra time that could mean the difference between your dog being taken or left behind.

There are effective alarm systems that can be fitted to kennel gates and doors but these are only effective if there is someone able to respond to the alarm should it go off.

Kennels are now being made in materials including fibreglass and plastic so it's worth looking at all the options of kennel systems before making a decision. Kennels need to provide warmth in winter and an equally desirable living environment in summer – and they have to be as secure as possible to keep the dog in and to keep unwanted visitors out.

## The house dog

Can a working gundog be kept as a house-dog? It's a question often asked – and the answer is yes, with a few provisos. The ideal scenario for the owner who wants to keep his working Labrador as a house dog is to ensure the dog has 'alternative accommodation' that can be used whenever necessary. For instance, a young working Labrador is like a sponge when it comes to learning and if allowed to always be a part of the hustle and bustle of family life it can undoubtedly lose focus. So while having a dog that spends a great deal of time with the family is acceptable, the dog either has to have a place of its own in the house or outside – somewhere it's happy to go and which is not considered in any way to be a punishment or seen as a place that creates a negative experience. Very young children and young Labradors can be a recipe for domestic mayhem simply because it's impossible to impose enough ground rules to prevent the dog coming under influences that can make training more difficult. In this situation an outside kennel is the best option although it's still important to allow the dog into the house whenever appropriate so that its upbringing will be well balanced and training can be undertaken with confidence.

So it's very much a case of working out a compromise so that the dog is brought up to know its job but is equally well mannered and respectful enough to spend time with the family. As a dog matures it may well be that it will have gained such a clear understanding of what it's role in life is that it will become totally unaffected by any of the unpredictabilities of family life but as a young dog, a safe haven to allow the dog it's own 'space' – more to benefit its mental state than anything else – is essential.

If an adult dog is spending part of its life kennelled and part in the house it's still very important to make sure that the kennel is of good quality. The advice on construction and insulation given previously should be followed even though the incumbent may only be a part-time lodger.

The routine of putting a house dog into its own space needs to be started from puppyhood so that as it matures it is perfectly accepting of how it fits into the family lifestyle. The biggest issue associated with keeping a working gundog in the house is that as youngsters they are bombarded with so many situations that kennel dogs don't have to cope with. And while many owners feel that keeping a working dog in the house is easier, it does require a more acute awareness of certain things. A dog kept in the house is living in a much kinder environment to one that's living in a kennel in terms of temperature so to suddenly plunge an adult dog from a centrally heated home onto a shoot for the day in the middle of winter needs undertaking with some consideration.

Training too needs some thought. After a training session a dog needs time to be left alone to assimilate what has been learnt – strange though that may seem but it's true. So a quiet place is important instead of simply bringing the dog back into an environment with all manner of domestic distractions. House dogs that are working gundogs can often feel like square pegs in round holes and those who decide to take this option of ownership have to do so with a large degree of give and take. A working Labrador will not be mincing around the park like a Poodle and come back into the house on tip-toes. It will be a large, sometimes rather smelly machine that has probably worked its heart out for you all day. So owners of working Labradors kept as house dogs have to be rather forgiving and remember that it was their decision to keep the dog as part of the family.

Nutrition has been covered in an earlier chapter but as far as the adult Labrador is concerned this is a dog whose dietary requirements should be under regular review depending on the age of the dog, the amount of work and/or exercise it's being given, the time of year and the environment in which it spends most of its time. But there are other factors that impart a more subtle effect on the body condition and health of the adult Labrador. Like humans all dogs are different and it's important to feed individual adult dogs according to their propensity for putting on weight. Some dogs are more of a type that burn up food much faster than others. These are

It's important to ensure hard working dogs are fed a high quality diet to meet their energy needs

the very active types and are the ones that can quickly lose condition in the shooting season or if kept in outside kennels with no additional heating in winter. I don't like to be able to count the ribs on a Labrador but it's not uncommon to find working Labradors in extremely lean condition. There is no need for dogs to be so 'light' and the assumption that it enables them to be more active or more efficient in their work is a fallacy. The truth is that Labradors kept in 'bare-ribbed' condition as I call it, are more likely to have less energy, work less efficiently and certainly be more prone to health issues simply because they are constantly in a state of negative energy. It's not good for male dogs and it can have a direct impact on fertility in bitches that are intended to be mated. The natural physiological process of any female animal living with an energy deficit is to 'shut down' its ability to breed – no female struggling to survive herself could cope with pregnancy or the production of offspring. So keeping bitches in 'fit but not fat' condition in the shooting season – and certainly not 'bare ribbed' – is essential.

One of the most notable characteristics of the Labrador, and something that was very much a part of its growth in popularity as a working dog with a love of working in water, was its double-coat. By that I mean the outer coat and the thick layer of undercoat that provides unbeatable protection from the cold and prevents water from reaching the skin. While this is still a trait desired in show-bred Labradors, it's one of the most important characteristics that have been lost from many working bloodlines. Shivering, thin-coated Labradors are not uncommon these days whereas at one time they would have been unheard of. Many owners of working Labradors who have never seen a dog with a true double coat but own the thin-coated type, need to be aware that these dog always require a higher level of feed to maintain them in good body condition and even more of a higher protein food during the shooting season or if engaged in a greater amount of physical exercise. These dogs have little insulation and burn up calories for fun, particularly in the winter months.

Without going over much of what has already been covered in the earlier chapter on feeding, it's important when making a choice about what to feed your Labrador, to be ready to make changes to the diet – in terms of amount fed and what nutritional value it's providing – relevant to your individual dog, the time of year and the activity he's engaged in. An 18% protein 11% fats/oils complete feed should be adequate for most Labradors that aren't working. Amounts fed can be stepped up from the

OPPOSITE PAGE Good nutrition and correct management ensures working dogs are maintained in tip-top condition

norm if necessary but if harder work is being undertaken or the dog is clearly not holding condition on this type of 18% ration, it will be necessary to increase it to say a 23% protein diet for at least one of his twice daily feeds.

Adult dogs go through many physical changes in their lifetime. The 12–18-month-old is often considered to be an 'adult' when in fact he is a teenager able to burn up calories required for growth and to fuel sheer physical exuberance. The middle-aged adult dog needs a diet that can be utterly relied upon to deliver a high standard of nutrition during the years when the dog is probably at its peak of physical effort. Swapping and changing diets isn't recommended for dogs of this age group and while one often hears owners say of their Labrador 'he'll eat anything' that can often be his downfall because an owner making a sudden change in the diet of a mature dog can find his enthusiasm is no guarantee that the 'new' food will agree with him or is good enough.

A lot of adult Labradors, particularly during the shooting season, do not look in good physical condition and that's largely because enough thought hasn't been given to their true dietary needs. There is no better advert for a dog food than finding someone whose dogs always look in top form and asking them what they feed!

Unless you are in the fortunate position to be able to spend a lot of time with your dog every day, exercise is something that adult dogs often lose out on. Unlike show-bred Labradors, those bred for work for the most part tend not to pile weight on even when exercise has to be restricted to fit in with the owner's lifestyle. Perhaps this is an opportunity to debate the issue of how much exercise an adult working Labrador needs? There are many working Labradors that are not exercised at all. They simply spend a short period every day in training and are then returned to their kennel. This regime is not one I agree with and while those that promote it believe that it keeps working dogs focussed on the sole purpose of their existence, I am more of the opinion that all work and no play makes Jack a dull boy. For many owners of working Labradors such an austere life-style is unlikely to factor into the way they want to own a dog but there is still a feeling that freedom to 'play' as part of the daily routine of a working Labrador serves to undermine its training. That I cannot agree with. All my dogs are given an opportunity – at least three times a day – to be allowed to run free. This would not be undertaken if there was any concern that they would not

respond to a re-call immediately. Yes, care has to be taken that – with young dogs in particular – temptations are not put in their way (rabbits, hares, cats or game) if their training hasn't encountered these. A degree of common sense has to prevail. Don't exercise working dogs where issues may arise that could undermine your training but by the same token don't keep a dog slammed up in a kennel on the assumption that if he never sees anything or gets to gallop freely he will remain steady and never 'take off' after a hare on a shoot day. Top trainers will no doubt disagree with my advice on this but I could not imagine owning dogs that could not be allowed to express the joy of freedom. In my experience the dogs with the biggest hang-ups are the ones who live solitary lives and never get a chance to let their hair down!

But moving on from this tricky subject and examining the need for exercise in adult dogs, I think we once again need to consider what we have got in a working Labrador. Not only is this a highly intelligent, biddable, kindly and genuine dog but it is also an athlete. Owners spend a

Working Labradors have to be physically fit enough to tackle any obstacle *(Photo: Sharon Rogers)*

great deal of time training working Labradors in an effort to achieve a high standard of mental awareness but tend to forget the physical demands of a working gundog. For the most part given regular exercise and training, an adult Labrador should be able to maintain a good degree of physical fitness but that will not be the case if the dog has to spend a fair part of his life kennelled and has a training or exercise schedule that is restricted – particularly during the week – because of the owner's other commitments.

As anyone who has been involved with hunting knows only too well, hunters may get part of the summer to recover from the winter's sport but well ahead of the autumn season they are brought up from grass and started on a fitness regime in readiness for the coming season. While the spring and summer can give working Labradors a well-earned rest – unless working tests are on the agenda – it's important not to assume that getting a dog ready for the shooting season means little more than cutting its food down by half during August!

Sprains, tendon injuries, cruciate ligament problems and bone breaks keep vets very busy but a lot of incidents with working gundogs could be avoided if dogs were always maintained 'match fit'. You only have to look at a good-sized Labrador clambering over a fence or wall with a large cock pheasant in its mouth to imagine the amount of physical strain that activity puts on to so many of the dog's muscles and limbs. So I think a bit more thought needs to go into addressing the fitness of working Labradors – and that doesn't mean keeping a dog 'bare-ribbed' – to ensure that they are in good enough shape to tackle any situation we may wish to put them into and to emerge from it successfully and without any physical stress or damage. And remember that these problems don't always manifest themselves immediately so a dog that lives a relatively sedentary lifestyle during the week but is then expected to kick-start and become a top class athlete at the Saturday shoot is obviously going to be more prone to problems. If time is tight it's far better to try to give a short amount of daily exercise rather than the occasional marathon. Building-up and maintaining a working gundog in good physical condition will not only avoid potential health issues from injury but will also impart a confidence in the dog and encourage him to tackle obstacles more adeptly. So often one sees a Labrador hesitating to jump a fence or tackle another obstacle and it's often because the dog doesn't feel capable of doing it, rather than a reflection of his inability or awkwardness.

Never underestimate just how much effort a working dog puts into his job *(Photo: Sharon Rogers)*

## Dog or bitch?

Dog or bitch – the vexed question? In many cases it's very much an individual choice. There are some who get on better with dogs and some who get on better with bitches. Those who prefer dogs like to think dogs are more honest and genuine; those who favour bitches believe them to be more devoted and focussed. The dog owning fraternity believe bitches to be intractable at times and as well as the inconvenience of coming into season – usually at the most inappropriate time of year – reckon they are harder to train and more selfish in nature. Bitch owners will say dogs can be more independent-minded, hot-headed, sometimes a bit stroppy with other males and are ever aware of the delights of the opposite sex.

Personally I don't believe dogs and bitches can be categorised so easily having had wonderful experiences with both over the years. What I do believe is that some people are more in-tune with either a dog or bitch and they should always remain loyal to their preferred choice.

Dogs expected to undertake a lot of water work will use up more energy than working on land *(Photo: Frank Toti)*

Those who own bitches can elect to have them spayed as a way of avoiding the inconvenience of a season and while vets will happily undertake this operation, there are some vets who say that to have a bitch spayed purely for the owner's convenience is inappropriate. So perhaps this is something that needs to be taken into consideration when deliberating over a dog or bitch pup.

# CHAPTER NINE

•

# Gundog Training – Laying the Foundation

W
HILE FIELD TRIALS continue to be the benchmark of excellence for assessing the skills of working Labradors, the vast majority of owners don't aspire to such elevated heights of competition. They simply require a Labrador to fulfil a role as a reliable shooting dog or one that's an effective member of a picking up team. These owners need a standard of training they can successfully apply and which will produce them a well-trained dog, but equally one that suits their particular needs.

The best field trial dogs can be awe inspiring in their work but to have such high standards – and the means of achieving such high standards – as the benchmark for the majority of owners of working Labradors has set the bar at a high level. The precise and almost robotic style of work that looks so impressive in competition is, in reality, an unattainable goal for most owners with lesser aspirations. Owners who feel they haven't achieved the best from their dog, or that their dog is simply failing in its ability to learn its craft, often find themselves in that position because the field trial training ethic is now widely applied as the cornerstone of all Labrador training.

It's important to keep the style of dog work seen at field trials very much in perspective and not to allow it to undermine lesser mortals among Labrador owners who may encounter training difficulties, often because they are trying to produce a different type of working gundog. Standards

Honing the ability of
a working Labrador to
hunt is a vital element
of its training

of training must always remain high – and field trial dogs are the epitome
of such standards – but there would be more confidence among new
owners of working Labradors if they could adopt an approach to training that was less pressured and less intense for both dog and handler. To
encourage training methods that produce working dogs for shooting and
picking-up that are more intuitive rather than robotic will achieve higher
standards among rank and file owners and engender greater confidence in
their training skills.

As we have already discussed, training a working Labrador must be
based on achieving a close 'connection' with the dog – something that
begins from the very first day of ownership. But having spent the early and

undoubtedly most formative months of the dog's life developing the first stages of the partnership, there comes a time when the nuts and bolts of building an effective working gundog have to be put in place. There is no specific age at which this needs to begin but most owners who believe they have a pup that is responsive and attentive to them, will instinctively know when 'pre-school' can actually start. I often think that it's indicative of not having developed a true rapport with a pup that forces owners to ask the question 'when should I start to do some proper training'.

Boisterous and unruly pups that are often considered to be in need of an early start to their training in an attempt to address their exuberance, usually end up being more problematic – both initially and in later life.

It's a simple case of the raw material not having received the correct grounding in terms of building any sort of rapport with its owner during puppyhood. At the other end of the scale the sensitive and quiet pup that hasn't benefitted from any confidence building by the owner will equally prove to be more of a challenge when asked to move into learning mode at the pre-school stage.

While there should be a seamless approach to moving into the stage of more formalised training, rather than suddenly introducing it, the same should apply to the way training progresses. There is no rigid 'age stage' that can be applied to training a Labrador; it's not a case of saying a dog is 12 months old so it should have achieved a certain standard of work by that stage. All dogs are different and all handlers apply training methods in a different way, but providing training is approached sensibly and correctly there should be a gradual progression that moves on as the dog clearly shows a readiness for the next stage or is obviously skilled enough to be taken out of its comfort zone and put into slightly more challenging situations. When novice trainers do find themselves facing problems it's usually because the dog has not fully grasped what it has been taught and there is an assumption that it is ready to progress when there is more of a need to re-affirm and consolidate what has already been learnt rather than go up a gear too quickly. It may seem monotonous to continue teaching a skill that you feel the dog has mastered but it will be of considerable value in the long term.

Taking training too quickly to try to get a young dog ready for the forthcoming season is not unusual. This is a situation when it would have been best to settle for a few odd days in January and save the dog for the

There is no rigid 'age stage' that can be applied to training – all dogs are different
*(Photo: Anne Taylor)*

following season. It's far better to take the long-term view and to look forward to many years of owning an accomplished working Labrador than years of having to cope with the shortcomings in the shooting field of a dog whose training was hurried.

## Pre-school

If you are genuinely uncertain about when to begin the first stages of formal training, it's worth seeking advice from someone with experience who should be able to evaluate you and your pup and decide when and how you should begin. When I feel the time is right for a pup to move onto the first stages of pre-school training I like to choose an occasion when the weather is good, a place that is quiet and free from distractions and at a time of day when I feel the pup is going to be at its most receptive. The middle of the day or early afternoon is a good time for training pups and

I always like them to have a few minutes to 'let their hair down' before we start so that the edge is taken off the pup's energy levels and to empty themselves so that I'm sure it's feeling comfortable.

## Early heelwork – the mechanics

By this stage I will have had a lead on the pup previously but I don't have hang-ups about heelwork as we have discussed in an earlier chapter. Because I am confident that the pup is in-tune with me the start of lead training is never a battle royal between us. So to begin with slip the lead on, give lots of praise, have treats in the hand and try and take a couple of steps back or to the side, encouraging the pup to follow. I only want the pup to take perhaps two steps towards me; that's all I want to achieve. If the pup objects to the lead, which it shouldn't if you give the right amount of encouragement and support, you need to let it get all that angst out of its system 'in situ'. If you encounter really serious objections from the pup you need to stand firm and just let it happen – don't add to the struggle by trying to overcome it. With the pup re-focussed on you again, you need to encourage the pup towards you with lots of positive praise. Keep the session short and providing you keep everything light and bright and avoid at all costs any pulling, jerking, tugging and chastisement, you will soon have a pup calmly walking a few steps towards you and then following you with a few more steps. You will get a sit-down strike from time to time but don't hoist the pup back on to its feet; simply go in a different direction – it always works!

Take it steadily and calmly and keep the pup focussed on you; soon you'll have a pup trotting along at heel and looking up at you and it will probably take no more than a couple of short sessions to achieve it. And if you've really connected with the pup you could achieve all of this in the first 10 minutes. And always keep the lead loose. I want a pup walking at heel with the lead literally hanging over the finger of one hand; the lead is a guide and no more; it's not an anchor or a tow-rope. Once we start to make real progress and I want the pup to turn with me at heel I may just make a slight contact through the lead, but if you can keep vocal contact and eye contact and keep the pup watching your hand to give added information about the direction in which you are about to go, the pup should turn and follow without the need to apply any directional pressure on the lead at all.

It should be possible to walk a dog at heel with the lead held lightly across two fingers – it's a guide not an anchor or a tow-rope!

BELOW Walking to heel is part of the training process and should evolve without applying pressure

I like to vary the pace of heelwork and I like to keep my body low so that the pup is looking at my face – that's something that really forges the contact. Marching along looking straight ahead and losing eye contact with the pup destroys the connection and leaves the pup open to drift away or pull forward. Once heelwork is progressing avoid boring square bashing; use twists and turns and give ample encouragement at all times – vocal and knee-patting to keep the pup close to you. It's amazing how quickly really tight turns can be mastered by pups and it keeps them on their toes so that they are never quite sure where the game is leading. And that's what it should remain – a game. It will all turn serious later on, but this is the time to get results based on the pup's raw and immature enthusiasm.

Walking to heel must *not* become the benchmark of having achieved a basic level of control that means you can now progress to some basic retrieves. Walking to heel is an organic part of the learning process and evolves and should improve in its correctness and style as the pup develops and you strengthen your working partnership. Frantic jerking and yanking at young pups in an effort to achieve precise heelwork in the early stages of training is dangerous and will undermine everything that follows. So allow heelwork to progress steadily as an ongoing part of the early training stages and don't feel it is a box that has to be firmly ticked before everything else can move forward.

## The sit

Training a dog to sit has always traditionally been achieved by applying pressure to the hindquarters and repeating the command 'sit'. I think I can honestly say I have no recollection of having to adopt this method and believe a far more effective approach can be achieved without having to make any hands-on contact with the dog at all. If your pup is as focussed on you as it should be, it should be possible to achieve a sitting position with sound, signal and correct body language. I start to practise some very rudimentary sitting when pups are probably about five months old; I'll start them in a pen or in the paddock with no lead on. If a pup comes up to me and I see an opportunity to achieve a sit I take it, but I make sure I keep it simple and give much praise. Once we embark upon training proper, and with a lead loosely on the pup I will attract the pup's attention, give a pip on the whistle, lift an open-palmed hand up and over the pup and say 'sit' with an emphasis

Keep the contact and the attention with hand tapping on thigh and vocal encouragement

on the 'S' sound. I keep the command low and calm and quiet. I use the open palmed hand facing downwards to achieve what I call 'putting a lid' on the pup so the hand needs to be at about waist height but over the pup. The pup should be looking at the open hand, hearing the voice command and at the same time your body languauage needs to be positive and affirmative so that you may appear to raise your upper body slightly over the pup to emphasise the message. If the pup moves backwards or to the side, continue the commands and all the other visual aids and a submission into a sit position will be achieved. Praise the pup – a stroke across the head or a rub on the chest. Properly trained this exercise will achieve a pup that will sit efficiently with the combined use of the repeated 'S' in 'sit' and the open palm visual command. That hand, you will soon find, is your most valuable piece of equipment. It has the ability to send messages, to guide at short distances to direct over long distances and to instruct. When a pup develops the correct level of awareness of the right hand of its owner and understands that it has a positive role to play in their relationship – and not one that delivers punishment – the rate of learning and progress is a joy.

## Be steady

Steadiness is an important message that has to be imparted to all working gundogs and the first stages of being steady – sitting and staying and being able to resist temptations – are important parts of the learning process. I cannot stress enough how critical it is *not* to try and achieve this by taking the pup to the edge of its comfort zone as a means of measuring success. Dogs that become unsteady are always those that have had bad experiences in the way they have been taught steadiness as pups. The relationship you are trying to achieve with your pup in order to nurture its desire to work as your partner for the rest of its life is one that I believe must be born out of trust and not one of fear. Sitting your pup and walking away from it is not an easy situation for a pup to deal with even if you have the correct rela- tionship. So any sit and stay exercises need to be short and they need to be successful. They do not want to take the pup into a zone that will trigger a 'break' in the stay; you should always err on the side of a short distance and repeated success to compound the message and confer on to the pup the

No need for jerking or pulling – a confident, happy pup at seven months off the lead and already learning his job

confidence that you are always going to come back even though you may be less than 10 strides away.

For all sit and stay exercises I put the pup into a sitting position by my side, slip the lead off quietly and use the open palm of my hand to maintain the 'lid' on the pup and give a clear visual message to 'sit and stay'; I give a single, short blow on the whistle to re-enforce the command and then, with my hand still keeping the 'lid' on I will say 'sit and stay'. I will not lose eye contact with the pup but will walk backwards keeping my open palmed hand at chest height. At any point at which I think the pup may break I stop walking backwards, repeat 'sit and stay' and may even take two steps confidently forward. Maintain the voice contact with repeated 'stay' and walk back to the pup, slip the lead on and praise. I don't want a pup to be 'whistled up' to me from the sitting position; this only confuses the issue because this was a sit and stay exercise and not a recall. What concerns me about many approaches in training classes is the assumption that all the pups are confident to line-up and be left. Every dog is different and steadiness exercises like this must be approached correctly from the start.

Pups that appear to be steady but are actually far from confident in that situation and have only achieved some degree of success by harsh re-enforcement by the handler, are often unsteady as adults. While discussing the very basic approaches to steadiness training I must advise avoidance of a training trick I have witnessed at some training clubs and which has no relevance to work in the shooting field other than to undermine a pup's confidence – and that is to leave a pup in the sit and stay position and then to approach it and walk around it. This is a futile activity that serves no purpose other than to make a worried pup even more so.

To take steadiness training a stage further I leave the pup in a sitting position with eyes on me. Initially I would keep a loose lead on the pup – if I am using a conventional gundog lead it would be 6ft in length – and would give the command stay or wait. When I feel the pup is focussed on me I would 'place' a dummy – not drop it – a few feet in front of the pup. It's likely that the first time this happens the pup will lurch forward to try and grab it but I would be ready with my lead to prevent contact being made with the dummy. I would repeat the same exercise over a period of time until I could actually drop the dummy in front of the pup and the pup would not make any attempt to move. You will be surprised that if this exercise is undertaken carefully a pup will quickly learn to be steady and

Using the hand to put a 'lid' on the sitting pup and accompanying it with a vocal 'sit'.

resist trying to pick up the dummy. Each time the exercise is performed successfully the pup must be praised. Take care with all praise at this early stage not to lavish it too heavily until the end of the session – individual praise must be enough to be recognised by the pup but not so much that it creates a breakdown of concentration and focus.

## On the hunt

Honing the ability of a working Labrador to hunt is a vital element of the dog's training and while pups should have a natural aptitude to do this, it's important to encourage it and for you, as the handler, to get involved at an early stage. While 'a good nose' is essential for a working Labrador to locate the game it has been sent to retrieve, it's important for the pup to learn from the outset that this is a job that involves both of you. How often do we see dogs in the shooting field who have a tremendous natural ability and determination to find game in the trickiest of situations and who demonstrate remarkable resilience and persistence – and yet they undertake their skills in a totally independent fashion that totally disregards any instruction from the handler.

Teaching a pup to hunt can be undertaken in various ways but by the time the pup is embarking upon the very early stages of formal training so far described, I like to have encouraged the hunting gene. This can be successfully undertaken anywhere and is all part of establishing the partnership and connection process. So with a five or six month-old pup playing in the garden or the paddock, and when it's preoccupied, I will hide three or four small dummies or tennis balls in some rough grass and then call the pup over. With lots of vocal and visual encouragement – and even an occasional hie-lost thrown in for good measure – I encourage the pup to get its head down. When concentration lapses I use my hands to direct the pup to an area close to one of the dummies and when we hit the jackpot I pile on the praise. It's all very casual and playful but it's sowing those first seeds of understanding in the pup that this is a co-operative venture that always comes up with the right result.

## No pressure

In the first few weeks of this early training stage everything must be kept light and bright and short – nothing too intense and nothing laboured to the point of resistance or utter boredom. Yes, training is all about building blocks but I am not of the opinion that you need to get every stage right before you move on to the next in these very early stages. The key is to build up the pup's confidence, enable the pup to adjust to the new degree of control that is being imposed on its lifestyle and most of all make sure there is success and positivity in all that you are engaged in as a partnership. Because the aim is to lay very broad foundations of learning at this pre-school stage, variety must be a paramount consideration to ensure the pup's mental development is maintained. But this is also very educational for the handler because by starting some elementary heelwork, some sits, some steadiness and enthusiastic hunting you are in a very strong position

The ultimate temptation – but steadiness is the benchmark of control

BELOW There comes a time when the nuts and bolts of training start to pay off

to make further judgments on the young pup's character, his propensity to learn and most of all his weaknesses.

You are also giving yourself a thorough insight into your pup's future role in life as a working gundog, something that will be of immense benefit as you progress to the next stage.

## Pre-school review

So easy heelwork with the emphasis on keenness to walk beside you and looking up at you (not creeping or cowering at your knee), some steadiness training designed to build confidence and not dangerously stretch his trust in you, some sits that are born out of body language more than body contact and some hunting for fun – these should form the basis of the first stage of pre-school training.

Everything should be undertaken to help make the pup succeed and if things that were going well suddenly start to go wrong, take off the pressure and go back to the beginning. Even though pups at this early stage may appear to be mopping up everything very quickly, there can be a hiccup in the learning process. Chastisement is a road to nowhere – it won't make what's been forgotten be remembered. Re-group and re-build and get the team seamlessly back on track.

•

# CHAPTER TEN

# Prep School

B Y NATURE OF ITS NAME the primary role of the Labrador Retriever in the shooting field is to retrieve game. But in the early stages the priority must focus on teaching the young dog not to retrieve – or more accurately, only to retrieve when it's told to. In other words, the fact that dummies are thrown and birds fall from the sky should not automatically trigger a response in the dog that these objects need to be collected and returned to the handler. It's very easy to allow the enthusiasm of a youngster to cloud good judgement and while it's certainly rewarding to see young dogs bounding out for a retrieve, it's important not to overdo this part of early training. The clear message must be that just because a dummy is thrown doesn't mean it has to be retrieved, but having said that the pup must also not be allowed to develop hang-ups about retrieving by allowing any of the efforts on the part of the handler to achieve control, to inadvertently introduce hesitation.

In general, but depending on how enthusiastic the pup is, I like to throw four or five dummies and allow the pup to retrieve only one of them. It's best to keep these sessions very short and work on the basis of gradually layering the message over time rather than driving it home with persistent lessons that end up having the opposite effect. Youngsters do vary in how much work you can give them but in the early stages just a few minutes is ample; in fact you can usually identify very clearly the point at which the attention span is starting to wane. Never go on too long and always end on a positive note no matter how trivial that may seem.

To improve steadiness I like to sit a pup in an area where I know I can quickly intervene if things go wrong, and start by dropping a small dummy or other objects from my training bag from about head height and from about three yards from the pup so that the object is very much 'in my space'. Only when the pup is remaining steady to items in my space do I look for steadiness to objects dropped closer to the pup but always remaining aware of not tempting providence and going too close. This is not about trying to get the pup to 'break' so that you can chastise it; it's about building confidence between you and the pup. During these exercises, which will ultimately lead to you being able to gently throw items to within two yards of the pup and even to roll tennis balls past the pup, it's important to give calm, vocal praise to instil the attitude of steadiness.

Our aim is to create a polished, efficient and controlled gundog whose retrieving skills have been honed from an inherent ability to do the job but to do it in unison with a handler and to respond to commands and instruction when in situations that test temptation to the hilt. Very few working Labradors don't retrieve as pups or youngsters. It does happen occasionally – and encouraging a reluctant retriever by giving it something personal to the owner to carry (a cap, scarf, or knotted handkerchief) is usually the first step in overcoming the problem.

The question so often discussed about early retrieving training is whether or not to allow a pup to 'run in'. Should you restrain the pup from the start of any retrieving training or should you throw a dummy and let the pup retrieve it? I don't like to embark upon any retrieving training that imposes restraint in the initial stage but that isn't to say that I encourage any sort of free-for-all attitude. What I really need to assess is how the pup is going to react if I throw a dummy. How keen is it? How confident is it to pick up the dummy and bring it back to me? How quickly does it do the job? Does it come around the side of me or land with a thump with unsophisticated enthusiasm in between my legs? Or does it take-off with it and start throwing it in the air and playing with it? All these assessments can be made with just one or two individual retrieves; and the way the pup reacts will affect how I proceed.

But no two pups are the same. I recall two littermates that were both very keen and adept retrievers from the very first day a dummy was thrown

for them, but the bitch was like a rocket on the outrun and the retrieve and thrust the dummy in between my legs when she brought it back. The dog went out steadily, picked it and brought it back at a good pace but far more methodically and presented the dummy to me carefully. I had the dog pup (at eight months old) steady to a thrown retrieve on the second lesson with no need to restrain him; the bitch pup, full of vim and vigour, needed to learn to contain her enthusiasm and had to be restrained initially until that lesson was learnt. Two litter mates, two very different retrieving skills.

If you hamper retrieving enthusiasm too early there's the risk that your efforts to 'be in control' can stifle keenness and may create hesitancy and questioning of something that is fundamental to the job the dog is going to be required to do. So don't get hang-ups about over control-ling pups; youthful enthusiasm can be harnessed later and fashioned into accomplished ability. So don't kill it, cultivate it.

Given that a youngster has the basic understanding of bringing back an item to the handler – and that the above assessment has been made – it's important to base the next stage in training around avoiding situations

Retrieving is what it's all about – but don't overdo it in the early stages of training where that inherent skill can be allowed to go awry. The aim is to develop a positive approach to all the training that follows by relying on success to achieve progress.

Retrieving in straight lines is important, not because we're trying to create an obedience-style Collie, but because it is the essence of control and giving direction. The faster and more efficiently a dog can be targeted on the shooting field to undertake a retrieve – say of a runner or a 'pricked' bird – the better. Achieving straight lines when the dog is sent away on seen or unseen retrieves is more difficult where a dog has not been used to this from the early stages of training.

So the first formal retrieving training should be undertaken in an enclosed space and preferably with a wall or fence-line or boundary hedge to maintain a degree of straightness in the outrun and the return. The enclosed space and the 'line' will more or less give the dog no other option than to come back directly to you in a straight line. Even a passageway can be made use of but if that's not available make sure the area you use provides you with maximum control over the exercise.

Use a track or a hedge or fence-line to help develop a straight out-run and delivery

The aim at this stage is to get a short, successful retrieve and ideally a good delivery. Concentrate on the dog; sit the dog by your side, talk to the dog and try and achieve a collected attitude. The pup isn't going to be allowed to run in so slip off the lead very carefully – you want to avoid the pup assuming that the lead coming off gives the signal to go – and restrain the pup but do this with the least amount of effort possible. With an assistant to help, the dummy should be placed where it can be clearly seen – and it may only be 10–15 yards away. I prefer to place a dummy at this early stage rather than throw a dummy because my aim is to get the dog going away and coming back, not marking the fall. And if a dummy is thrown it only serves to heighten the excitement and at this point I want a calm and controlled exercise.

Keep the pup calm and maintain the 'hold' until the moment you feel there's a degree of submission to your control. The aim is for the pup to leave your side on whatever command you have selected to 'trigger' that forward propulsion. Some prefer to use the name of the dog, others will say 'get on' or 'get out'.

Don't undertake long distances for marked retrieves in the early stages

Once picked there should be lots of praise and encouragement from the handler as the dummy is brought back and presented to you, but the position you adopt to receive the dummy from a young dog is possibly even more critical than ever at this stage of training. It's important to present an 'open frame' to the returning pup but very often handlers appear very 'closed' and unwelcoming to a pup with a retrieve. Very often any reluctance to come in can be attributed to being somewhat daunted by the upright stance of the handler or the body language.

So don't hesitate to get down on your haunches for those early retrieves if it means accentuating the welcome and creating a 'safe-haven' situation for the dog.

Some young dogs may drop their heads at the point of delivery – a habit often caused by sheer embarrassment. Silly though that may sound it is very often the case.

If you believe the pup is genuinely embarrassed or shy try to avoid looking directly at the pup but give lots of encouragement – tapping the chest or any movement that breaks the pup's preoccupation with being rather coy about coming in to you should be tried. If necessary get the pup to stand up on its hind legs and jump up at you with the dummy if that's what it takes; all these habits can be sorted out later but at this stage I want the pup and the dummy as close to me as I can get them.

The display of 'embarrassment' can often be caused by the pup simply being so proud of its effort to do the job for you that it can barely complete the exercise. So be patient about this bashful enthusiasm and all will come right in time. Far better than to try and focus on it as a problem – which it's unlikely to develop into anyway.

There's always a debate about whether a dog should learn to present the dummy in a sitting position or simply present the dummy while still standing. I think it's very much up to the individual dog and the handler. If too much emphasis is placed on requiring a 'sitting' position, it can become an issue and detract from what we're actually asking the dog to do. Focussing too much on a 'sit' can confuse a young dog and often leads to the dummy being dropped either when the dog is in front of the handler or just a yard or so before it reaches the handler. The sole aim at this early stage of training is to get the dog coming back to you with enthusiasm and self-satisfaction that the job has been done. I want a lively retrieve and the dummy brought back to me so that I don't have to move from where I am standing to take it from the dog. But to help encourage young dogs to come in close with the dummy and to come back with verve it's important to send all the right signals to the dog on its approach to you.

The dog will come back with more gusto to an 'open' handler than to one who is less so. For young dogs at this stage the arms should be held wide, even the legs can be apart – all with the primary purpose of sending a welcoming message to the dog and providing a target. At the same time there should be plenty of visual and vocal encouragement and for me that means pips on the whistle and calling the dog's name – even clapping my hands if necessary. The retrieve is fundamental to all training and it's essential to get it right from the start.

While it's best if early retrieves are undertaken in the enclosed space suggested, if the handler can stand with their back to a wall or fence it will avoid pups developing the habit of going around the side of you and even trying to get behind you with the dummy. If there is a tendency for a pup to go alongside you don't make a big deal about it. Resist putting out an arm to grab the dog as it slips alongside; all this does is make matters worse. If the dog does bypass the target just give lots of encouragement to bring it back to where it should be. You will get a correct delivery eventually but rough treatment and trying to achieve perfection from day one will dig you deeper into more problematical training issues.

For something as basic as the retrieve – in terms of the dog's natural ability to undertake it and the handler's skill in training – it's surprising that a lot of dogs have retrieving and presentation issues. Many are the result of incorrect training at a very elementary stage or, to be more precise, a lack of awareness on the part of the handler about what is actually going on in the dog's mind during this exercise. The 'embarrassment' we have just discussed is symptomatic of sensitivity and is something that needs a sympathetic approach to overcome it in the correct manner.

If you start to ask for too much at the point of delivery other issues can creep in like dropping the dummy/bird before it's taken. Don't be in a hurry to take the retrieve. The dog must be allowed its moment of glory and left to relish holding its 'prize' for a few very important seconds before the handler attempts to take it. Hurried removals of the retrieve lead to dogs spitting out the dummy or standing back instead of presenting it. So let the dog savour its success, give lots of praise so that the dog clearly understands that what it has done is exactly what you wanted it to do and that you are hugely proud of its efforts. Stroke the dog gently on the head, give lots of praise and use the other hand to slip gently under the chin almost as a sort of safety net to keep the dummy where it is – but just for a few seconds. On the command 'leave', given encouragingly and not threateningly, the dog should release the dummy. And then give more praise because this pup has just given up something that was very important to it and it must be acknowledged. So many problems with retrieving are caused by rushing this most fundamental part of training.

Once the dog has learned to be steady it's time to start retrieving dummies that have been thrown. Again, this is often introduced more effectively with the help of an assistant. It means you can focus on the dog and your body language can remain unchanged rather than infused with the energy needed to throw the dummy and possibly break the dog's concentration and risking a run-in. Once you feel a degree of steadiness has been achieved this is an exercise you can undertake single-handedly but in the initial stages it's more valuable to you as a handler to focus on the dog.

Don't undertake long distances for marked retrieves in the early stages. These may seem like simple exercises for your pup but you must be aware of all the elements you are now introducing and how the young dog has to learn to 'compute' all of them at the same time. The dog is being asked to sit by your side and be steady, to watch (but not move) when the dummy is thrown and to mark its fall, to remain still until you give the command and then to undertake the out-run and the retrieve. Quite a lot for a young dog to take in all at once and something that we tend to overlook.

Just before the dummy is thrown some handlers like to give the command 'mark' as a signal to the dog that it has to 'mark' the fall of the dummy. It's a good addition to the armoury of commands but it must be delivered in a quiet tone that must not in any way suggest to the dog anything other than what you are asking it to do. Sometimes the utterance of any word when a young dog is sitting steady can trigger a run-in. And it's important to achieve the right balance of eye contact at this point; if you keep your eyes fixed on the dog it means you don't know where the dummy has fallen but very often dogs will also remain transfixed on the handler at this point – awaiting the command to be sent for the retrieve – but in so doing fail to mark the fall of the dummy. So steadiness must be achieved without the need for the handler to keep a fixed gaze on the dog.

Once the dog is steady and marking retrieves and undertaking the retrieve correctly, don't be in too much of a hurry to start lengthening the distance or throwing dummies into cover. Consolidate success rather than push the boundaries too early and encounter a problem. There is no better foundation than building up a dog's self-confidence. Yes, progress is important and has to be a part of the training process but don't be concerned that the dog may be getting bored; far better to get bored but master his craft in the process rather than put the dog in a challenging situation too soon.

Once the pup is retrieving confidently it's time to see how it responds to fur and feather. Wrapping rabbit skins around canvas dummies and attaching pheasant wings (or the wing feathers that can be bought from gundog training equipment suppliers) should have given the pup the first 'taste' of what it's like to have something other than canvas to retrieve. I know some people give quite young pups a partridge or even a small hen pheasant (partly thawed from the deep freeze or fresh) to retrieve in the belief that the pup needs to have the experience without delay – possibly because they feel the pup may have a problem with game if it's not introduced early

Rabbit skins and pheasant pelts help the transition from canvas dummies to game
*(Photo: Sporting Saint)*

enough. Of course no one wants to leave it too late and end up with a problem, but once I feel a pup is confident and not likely to do something silly with a dead pheasant I will introduce one. Initially I will place the bird some distance away – definitely don't throw it – and then send the pup. Nine times out of ten there will be a few seconds of inquisitive sniffing and perhaps even rolling over the bird with the nose – I don't mind the sniffing but once that natural line of enquiry has passed I want the bird brought back to me so I start to whistle and give all the encouragement I have to do in order to get the job done. I may repeat it once more but not more than that for the first session. There is always a tendency for this new and rather exciting object to trigger a playfulness in pups on the first day game is introduced to training and my advice is to quit while you are ahead.

Other game – either fresh or from the freezer – can be used in training in place of dummies. And it can be useful to either have a range of game species in the freezer or try to obtain them fresh if the shooting season is underway to help the pup learn that there is a lot more to life than simply retrieving pheasants.

## Your right arm

The position and use of the right arm as a signal to send the dog forward is worthy of discussion. While it's important to give a young dog as much help as you can as you send it away from you for those early marked retrieves, the position of the arm and the hand do seem to create issues for some novice handlers. If the flat hand is positioned very close to a young dog's head it's not unusual for the dog to focus on the hand. As soon as the hand is moved away the dog either jumps in the air looking for it or is hesitant to go forward. While the hand on the end of the outstretched arm is an essential part of early training it's important not to use it so that the dog becomes too transfixed on the hand. I like to keep the arm and hand slightly above and to the side of the dog's body so that the forward movement of the hand to give the signal to go forward is a swift and momentary movement and not one that lingers in front of the dog's nose.

Of course there are those who say a dog doesn't need any hand signal as an additional aid to a voice command to be made to go forward for a marked retrieve on the assumption that the dog has seen the fall. This school of thought believes that directional hand signals from the handler

The position of the right hand at the point of sending the dog forward is important

should only be given as a means of directing the dog to go out for an unseen retrieve – in which case the arm is an essential means of giving direction and guidance.

## More difficult retrieves

Satisfied that retrieving training on marked dummies is progressing well it's time to start adding to the repertoire by throwing a dummy into deeper cover to encourage the dog to hunt and by introducing double-marked retrieves – one to the right and one to the left. Keep distances within the dog's capability at the start and go back to the enclosed area if necessary to give you more control if things go wrong. Double retrieves, which simulate a situation in the shooting field of two birds down, one of which needs to be picked as a priority, are most effectively taught if the handler makes the most use of body language in the early stages. With the dog sitting and steady I start by throwing a dummy to the right; once it has landed and the dog has marked the fall I give the command 'leave that'; I give the command forcibly by voice to make my request very clear. I then turn my body slightly to the left and in so doing not only use my body so that it's in the correct position to accentuate my action of throwing the second dummy to the left, but it also serves to create a 'mental' block to the dog concerning the first dummy. When the second dummy has landed I repeat the 'leave that' command. I then straighten my stance giving it a slight right-handed angle with the intention of switching the dog's body balance to the right; when the dog is balanced to the right, its vision is to the right and I am looking to the right. Using my outstretched right arm and hand as the directional aid I then signal to the dog to affect the right-handed retrieve. Once correctly delivered there is then a big risk that a young dog will shoot off for the second dummy without being instructed. So it's important that as soon as you have taken the dummy you achieve control of the dog by voice and to return it to the sit position. Use a firm voice and give a positive command to re-affirm control of this tempting situation for a young dog. With the dog by your side you can then send it for the second dummy.

Once this double retrieve has been mastered it can be taken to another level by re-throwing the first dummy after it has been retrieved, giving the 'leave that' command and then sending the dog for the second. The remaining dummy can then be retrieved by hand or the dog can be sent.

Taking the basic elements of what the dog has learnt so far can be applied to various other training situations. While you are walking the dog at heel you could then throw a dummy well ahead of you and suddenly stop. The dog should similarly stop or be taught to do so. You are simulating a situation either rough shooting or during a walked-up drive where game could be flushed in front of you and you require an instant reaction from the dog.

Similarly the dog must be taught how to react to another bird falling close by when he is in returning to you with a retrieve. Start this exercise by throwing the 'distraction' dummy when the dog is getting close to you on his return with the retrieve and try and position yourself so that you can block his path if he shows any tendency to divert away to collect it.

When I throw the diversion dummy I usually give a grumpy 'No' command making it clear to the dog that what it has just seen has connotations of 'leave well alone'. As this exercise progresses the diversion dummy can be thrown further away and even closer to the dog to build up his ability to resist and to remain focussed on the job in hand.

At this point it's important to stress that even as training moves up a gear the natural progression must also be developing a close bond of understanding between the dog and the handler. At all stages the level of 'connection' must be deepening so that the handler is receiving clear signals from the dog that a relationship is evolving. I don't like to see dogs that are clearly not at one with their handlers before a training session and then are put through a series of 'pony tricks' in a very clinical fashion that indicates the dog has learnt what to do but is going through the mechanics of the exercise rather that demonstrating any real working partnership with the handler.

Use repetition, familiarity and hedges or fences to improve speed and straight lines when training for unseen retrieves

Training a dog to leave you and find something with no prior knowledge of where that object is can be a tall order for some dogs that simply lack the confidence in themselves and don't fully believe what the handler is telling them. That's why it's so important to build on success and total trust in all things that have gone before this stage.

In the shooting field by far the most birds a dog will have to retrieve, particularly if it's a picking-up dog, will be those it hasn't seen fall. So hunting skills, the ability to take directions and respond to the stop whistle are all required in this part of a dog's training. A dog needs to be confident enough to leave the handler when instructed and to go in the direction that your hand signal has indicated. But in the early stages of training on unseen retrieves the dog must quickly find what it has been sent for – and it's up to the handler to make sure that can happen without too much effort on the part of the youngster. Repetition and familiarity must be used to advantage in this exercise so select a place where regular 'marked retrieves' have been undertaken and make sure you are aware of the wind direction. The dog will make full use of any scent it can detect to locate effectively an unseen retrieve so you need to make sure that the wind direction is working in the dog's favour and bringing any scent from the hidden dummy towards the dog.

Making sure you are in an area with which the dog is familiar to bolster his confidence and with an assistant on hand, start with a couple of straightforward seen retrieves so that the young dog has a clear understanding of what's wanted. Then, while distracting your dog's attention, ask your assistant to place a dummy in an area close to where you have been sending the dog for marked retrieves, making sure that you are sending your dog into the wind so that he can take full advantage of scent. Be mindful of keeping the distance short – possibly shorter than you have been using for marked retrieves – because you want the dog to get into the area where the dummies are hidden quite quickly and almost to be 'on the case' before he has had time to question the fact that he has actually left you, gone away from you and yet has no idea why other than he has followed the instruction. Issues with unseen retrieving usually emanate from a situation where the dog is sent too far away from the handler, that no account has been made of the wind direction and that the dog loses focus too quickly. The essence of unseen retrieves is to build up in the dog's mind the belief that he will always be successful in finding something when you have sent him. He has total belief in you.

I prefer to use one dummy but some prefer to put out several on the basis that the dog will quickly get a result. The issue can be that the dog may locate a dummy but then 'wind' a second and so the exercise starts to fall apart as he tries to retrieve both. Once the dog is in the area where the dummy has been hidden the handler can encourage the dog to 'hunt' with the command 'hie lost' – although don't give commands excessively because they may serve more to distract the dog rather than encourage it.

In the early stages of training for unseen retrieves young dogs should not have to work too hard to be successful; as this exercise is extended into longer distances and perhaps a fence or ditch has to be negotiated en-route, it's important at all stages of the training to maintain the dog's momentum in going forward in the firm belief that he will 'find'. So as distances are extended, and to avoid the annoying habit of dogs going 30 yards and then stopping to ask for reassurance, it's worth keeping voice contact to maintain forward propulsion with an occasional 'get on' or 'get out' just to keep the engine running and maintain the dog's commitment to the job.

Young dogs benefit from working in the presence of others once the basic rudiments of training have been achieved

Trained properly and ensuring that a dog is never chastised for failing on an unseen, this is one of the most fundamental and most useful of training skills a dog has to master. The essence of success is to instil total and unquestioning belief in the dog's mind that when you send it on an unseen retrieve it will, often with your help through direction, find what it has been sent for. And if there is a river to cross, a wall to be scaled or any other obstacle in its path to be overcome, you can be assured your dog will do its very best in that situation.

Encouraging dogs to travel long distances for unseen retrieves is best achieved by allowing a dog to see a dummy dropped and then taking the dog in a straight line away from it – up to 100 yards if the dog is confident. If this is done in a field with no distraction the dog will have less opportunity to lose concentration. Once the distance has been reached, turn, sit the dog and then send it. Repeat this exercise a few times each day over the long distance for at least a week and then try letting the dog see two dummies dropped. Always use the same field. The dog will certainly go back for one dummy with enthusiasm but it may, at first, be a little hesitant about the second. Give the dog every encouragement and chances are that by the time it has got 40 yards from you the penny will have dropped and the second dummy will be on its way back to you.

Progress to the stage when a single retrieve can be undertaken in the same format but then – and you may need an assistant here – send the dog for a second dummy that it hasn't seen. By now the dog should be well used to taking the route across the field for the dummy it knows is there; this time it hasn't seen a second dummy left but repetition should overcome doubt and because the dog has faith in you and what you have asked it to do it should undertake the second retrieve almost on 'auto-pilot' and successfully deliver the dummy.

## Runners and rabbit pens

It always amazes me that we spend time teaching young dogs not to go near poultry and not to chase rabbits and hares and yet there will come that first day – although be in no rush with a youngster – when that large cock pheasant will hit the ground and take off like an Olympic sprinter. Suddenly all those months of steadiness training and all those firm words to dissuade interest in anything feathered that moves on the ground, have to be put on one side because now you want this dog to take off in haste and return triumphant with a live bird and with barely a feather out of place. A tall order I always think – and yet these dogs have the ability to decide what they are allowed to 'chase' and retrieve and what they aren't. But putting dog psychology aside for a moment, let's discuss the issue of runners. Young dogs must not be allowed to take runners before they are confident retrievers that are able to quickly and precisely cope with a large, live gamebird and not only to retrieve it successfully but also to do so with no injury to themselves or the bird. It's not really something you can train for other than to avoid putting your dog into a situation before it's really ready. But when there is an opportunity that you feel is right – say the bird is a pricked handy-sized hen pheasant with a bit less 'puff' than most – that's probably the ideal opportunity to start.

Rabbit pens can be hired in most areas and are a boon for quelling the enthusiasm of young dogs. Rabbit pens with rabbits and poultry should be visited as often as necessary until your dog has become totally inured to fur and feather. You will probably have to make it quite plain with some

Young dogs benefit from time in a rabbit pen and need to learn the difference between poultry and game

On a shooting day the emphasis needs to be on the efficient and safe delivery of the game

severe tones that the incumbents of the pen have 'nothing to do with you'; if you have the correct relationship with your dog you will know the point at which he has become de-sensitised to these creatures and at that point, you should be able to practise some simple retrieves. Never underestimate the value of time spent in a rabbit pen as a part of early training.

And there is also the popular training aid of a rabbit-skin dummy on an elasticated line. This is a two-handed job but can really bring some genuine temptation into training situations as the dog develops its ability and becomes more committed to its task.

## When things go awry

Gundog training is never plain sailing and problems and crises will occur. Taking the education of your young dog as a stage by stage process and making sure the dog isn't made to feel pressured or insecure should help to avoid some of the training issues that can suddenly bring things to a halt. The dog that 'sings' is a problem, no one needs vocal accompaniment on shoot day so 'whining' tendencies must be tackled. There are all manner of ways of attempting to do this but I have to say that while some will say they have cured a dog of whining when working, it can be a very tricky fault to correct. The way the pup has been managed as well as the way he has been trained are, in my opinion, the most likely causes of whining. A dog whines to release nervous energy and that may be because he finds it's hard to remain in a 'collected' frame of mind when he is expected to sit and be still and silent or it may be because his training has been 'high energy' rather than solid, affirmative and calm. Whatever the cause it's unacceptable. Correcting the dog immediately a whine is heard is the most widespread approach – this can either be by voice, by jerking the lead if the dog is on the lead or some even squirt the dog with water. While some of these methods may achieve a degree of success I would advise anyone with a youngster that's displaying this tendency to seek professional advice rather than tackle it themselves and possibly make matters worse. An experienced trainer should be able to assess the dog and assess you as the handler – only then can an appropriate course of action be taken. Whining dogs are dogs 'on the edge' and it doesn't take much to tip them over. There are of course dogs that have a habitual whimper or even a nervous 'yawn' with a slight squeak at the end. While not whiners in the true sense of the word they are still showing signs of uncertainty and expressing nervous energy. No gundog should whine or yawn or whimper so if this is a problem it's best to bring in an expert to try and save the day.

Hard-mouthed dogs are another problem that may be encountered and again, this is a fault that can usually be traced back to training and very often even further back than that. It's often likely that something happened to a pup during the time it was growing up and before training started that may have triggered a tendency to develop a harder grip with its mouth. So be very careful about the way anything is taken from the mouth of a young dog – and if the dog is part of the family that rule has to be adhered to by all even when the pup has hold of a very expensive pair of shoes. Never pull, tug or prise anything from a pup's mouth. Deal with the situation calmly and provided you have a bit of patience the item will be given up without a struggle. If a pup is sharing it's life with an older dog there's a very good chance that tug of war games are a very popular pastime – and therein lies the first stages of teaching a dog how to be hard-mouthed. Any hint that a dog is becoming hard-mouthed by the way he may be reluctant to give up a retrieve in training needs addressing, but again no pulling or tough treatment. The dog is holding on hard because something has happened to it to suggest that what it has will be taken away and that is not what the dog wants to happen. What you have to instil into the dog is firstly that you are pleased it has brought the retrieve back to you but you must then diffuse the situation if there is any tension and allow the dog to release the dummy gently. Very often hard-mouthed tendencies are the result of a dog being far from relaxed in his work and the grip is a sign of tension. So take some of the pressure off the dog, go down a gear with his training and keep things simple and straightforward for a while in the hope that he will become less anxious and more relaxed in his delivery.

# CHAPTER ELEVEN

·

# The Next Level

BEING ABLE TO CONTROL a Labrador from a distance is as essential to someone working a Labrador as part of a picking up team, or even as a peg dog, as it is to someone competing in a test or trial. To the novice working on dummies it can look impressive when it's been mastered by the dog, but on a shooting day when a dog has to be stopped after being sent for a dead bird and switched quickly to take a strong runner heading in the opposite direction, it's an essential skill. So teaching directional training is not about 'pony tricks', it's a much needed and practical part of any working Labrador's education. Surprisingly it isn't difficult to achieve provided it's tackled in the right way and you have made sure the dog is 100% on the 'stop' whistle to ensure that you have those vital few seconds to halt the dog, grab his attention and give him the required direction command.

Just as throwing a dummy at the very beginning of training a dog to retrieve can add a frisson of excitement that can increase the risk of a young dog running in, so too with initial directional training. So 'placing' the dummy on the ground rather than actually throwing the dummy into the position from which you want the retrieve to take place should help to eliminate the risk of running in. Remember that for many young dogs this is the first time it's being asked to undertake a command where you are not by its side which can give some dogs an opportunity to abuse their sudden independence.

The first stage of directional training involves sitting the dog with its back against a fence or wall. The dummy to be retrieved needs to be about 10 yards or so to the side of the dog (I prefer to choose right to begin with) so I leave the dog in the sit and stay position and I walk away and quietly put the dummy down in full view of the dog and in a position parallel with the line of the fence or wall so that the dog travels in a straight line to undertake the retrieve. I will then position myself about 10 yards in front of the dog. I re-affirm the sit and stay with a whistle command (single blow) and a visual command by holding up my right arm, palm flat and facing the dog; but be careful to keep the visual command at no higher than face height and close to the body. Confident that the dog is steady the arm can then be moved and outstretched purposefully to the right and the appropriate command given. I use the dog's name in the same way that I would use the dog's name for other momentum-driven commands. The retrieve should follow and be correctly presented. That is the basis of directional training – creating a situation in which all the physical elements are designed to help the dog. The wall or fence behind creates the structure to prevent the dog going back and encourages the dog to move in a straight line when the command is given.

Using that as the basis, the permutations are many as the dog gains in confidence but I would urge all training to progress first on right-handed retrieves and then on left. If you begin by throwing the dummy and the dog runs-in the tendency is to correct the dog for his mistake and repeat until he gets it right, correcting all the time he gets it wrong. This tactic only serves to extend the learning time by almost forcing errors instead of adopting an approach that will enable the dog to learn this skill from a win-win method where the trainer will progress by building confidence in the dog. Putting a dog in a situation where it is more likely to make a mistake and using error as a basis for learning is pointless. So once the dog is steady and has grasped what you are asking it to do based on a dummy that has been placed you can then go up a gear and try throwing a dummy into the same position – but do it with as little fuss as possible. Once this stage is mastered, the distance the dummy is thrown can be increased and the distance you stand in front of the dog can be increased. Of course as in all exercises there is inevitably the risk of dogs starting to pre-empt a command and many dogs can do this before the actual directional signal is given. So once the dog has become almost over-confident it's time to either place the dummy or throw

Give clear hand signals for directional training

the dummy and then for the trainer to manually pick-up the dummy just to ensure that the dog doesn't assume that he knows what he's got to do before he's even asked to do it. Clever dogs soon learn to be a step ahead. It shows intelligence not a failure to learn so make sure the dog knows that he can't always second guess what's coming.

Once right-handed retrieves have been perfected it's time to replicate the regime for left-handed retrieves. I like to do all this training in the same location so that it helps to compound the learning process. Just taking this exercise to the next level – and still maintaining the location – a dummy can be thrown to the right and another thrown to the left. The dog will mark both of course. You must then, before you give the command for whichever dummy you require, be assured that you have the dog's 100% focus on you. There is a point at which you should be able to 'read' the dog in terms of its expression and body position; if you want the right hand dummy and you

The dog has to learn what the direction is telling it to do

think the dog will go left (particularly if the left dummy was the last one thrown) you must wait until you have the dog's attention focussed on you, watching your body language as well as your visual direction. Lean your body and head towards the right and give a clear right-handed signal with arm outstretched. Dogs that go for the wrong dummy at this stage most often make the mistake because the handler hasn't waited long enough to 'connect' mentally with the dog and allowed the dog to relax, failing to watch the handler's body language. If this double direction exercise is rushed it fails; giving the dog time to assimilate all the mental influences it's under and make the correct decision can take a bit of time so allow the dog to do this and get it right. Once learnt it means directional training can be moved into a more open location and progressed in terms of distance without the support 'framework' of a wall or fence.

A keen response to a directional command

## 'Get back'

This is a relatively straightforward exercise to undertake but it's important from the outset to achieve straight lines in the way the dog applies the command. Trained in an open situation allows opportunities for the dog to 'waver' and a need to be brought back on-line with directions and that shouldn't necessarily be required. So it's again important to begin this exercise using the definition of a fence or wall to provide the straight line that will guide the dog. Walking with the dog at heel you should come to a halt and the dog must sit. Throw the dummy a few yards ahead of you and in line with the boundary you are working alongside. Then turn with the dog at heel and walk back from where you came – probably about 10 yards or so. Sit the dog and, for the first few times this exercise is undertaken I prefer to walk backwards a few yards to maintain eye contact. I also re-affirm the sit and stay with a raised hand, palm open and I keep the hand in that position. I do this not only to ensure the dog remains steady but also because some dogs pre-empt the get back visual command as soon as the arm is moved; by keeping the dog fixed on the raised arm as a command to 'sit and stay' reduces the risk of this happening. As with all these training methods the intention should be one of applying approaches that avoid the dog making errors or developing faults, rather then letting the dog fail and then needing to correct the failure when it could have been avoided.

With the dog sitting a few yards in front of you and with your hand raised you must wait for the dog to be totally focussed on you at which point you should then 'flick' the hand – in a gesture of sending the dog away from you – and at the same time give the voice command 'get back'. The dog should turn and undertake the retrieve. As the dog becomes more proficient the distances can be increased and then of course the exercise can be progressed to a situation where the dog doesn't see the dummy left so he is being asked to 'get back' for an unseen retrieve.

Once you are confident that the 'get back' – for both seen and unseen retrieves – can be moved out into a more open situation be mindful of the location. Certainly in the early stages it's worth helping the dog to maintain and develop its ability to keep to straight lines by using situations that help guide the dog; he may not realise that he is keeping to a straight line but by some planning on your part you can orchestrate this.

## Hunting in an area

This is often something that has a reputation for being difficult to train for but how quickly a dog can master this aspect of his work very much depends on how responsive he is to you. To begin with undertake this piece of training in an area in which you can quickly take hold of the situation and address any tendency to ignore you. Nothing will be learnt by the dog if everything ends up in a shouting match simply because you are too far away to do anything more effective. In essence the aim is to send the dog away from the handler into an area in which there is game to be retrieved. We know the area but not the precise location of the game so the handler's task is to keep the dog focussed and hunting in the area until the game is located. The risk is always that the dog may take off in another direction thinking he knows better than the handler – the aim must be to keep control of the dog at a distance and to keep him hunting. In training for this and where the area is not far away and relatively small it may not seem too challenging but if you're on a shoot day or in a trial, dogs need to be able to perform this skill very long distances from the handler and yet be as responsive and accurate as though they were 20 yards away. So that's why it's essential to have a dog 'on the button' in terms of the stop and his ability to respond to directions and to get his head down and hunt when told to.

Begin by putting a dummy into cover say 40 yards away and leave the dummy to the far right of the area. Send the dog into the area but send him to the far left. Hopefully the dog will have learnt a whistle command for hunting (for me it's a short followed by a longer blast which is repeated) when the dog has reached the far left hand side of the 'area' whistle him to stop and gain his attention and then give him the signal to hunt; add plenty of vocal encouragement and if he starts to drift to the right whistle him to stop, draw him back to the left and get him hunting again. Whenever he seems to be drifting use your controls to bring him back, always avoid-ing the far right-handed area until you feel the time is right to draw him over with a right-handed signal and to hopefully locate the dummy to be retrieved. The key to this piece of training is making sure the dog is listen-ing to you and that he doesn't get so totally absorbed in hunting that he loses focus. In training the initial purpose is teaching the dog to stay in the area you want him to work in more than instantly finding the game. On a shoot day the aim is to find the game and retrieve it as quickly as possible

ABOVE Once the dog has grasped directional training in an enclosed space, move into a more open area

But if things need reaffirming don't be afraid to shorten the distance to regain the dog's confidence

but to do that may mean working an area of thick cover very thoroughly and that's where the persistence and commitment of hunting a particular area as directed by the handler must be accomplished. Holding a dog in an area on a shoot day or at a trial when there is so much game scent around can be one of the most challenging pieces of work for dog and handler but use should always be made of the wind and the dog should be handled into the wind to give him all the help he needs to succeed.

## Jumping

In my experience some Labradors are natural jumpers and some aren't – but even the less accomplished can have their skills honed to cope with most obstacles provided they aren't asked to leave their comfort zone too early. Clearly it's very important not to allow young Labradors to jump any obstacles while their bones are still soft and any jarring of the joints can lead to health issues, particularly in the elbows. We are very strict about not allowing youngsters to jump anything until at least 12 months old. In many

Accomplished jumpers make light work of early jumping training

cases it can be difficult preventing the keen jumpers to keep all four legs on the ground if they come across something that they find too irresistible not to jump over; but my advice would be not to assume that a dog is ready to jump just because it shows a propensity for it.

Jumping needs to start with a very low height of about two feet. Ideally this should be in a situation where the dog has no option but to get over the obstacle and with you stepping over it first – and with an older dog to give a lead if possible – the youngster should follow. While some young dogs 'fly' a fence and don't touch it at all, others (and very often in the early stages) do like to scramble over or at least make contact with the obstacle with their front feet. So make sure the jump is secure and doesn't wobble. Ideally a top rail – round-wooden fence post is ideal – with chicken netting

Young dogs need to jump across ditches as well as over obstacles

beneath is a good combination although you may need to make sure the netting is fully visible to the dog so that it doesn't go charging through it! Any training jump must be constructed so that there is no risk of a dog injuring itself or getting a leg stuck. Safe and solid are the watchwords for constructing training jumps.

Once a young dog has been allowed to jump and is confident, the next job is to introduce a command to jump, to develop skills over higher levels and then to learn how to develop a technique while carrying a dummy and ultimately game. The command 'over' is the most widely used as the command to jump an obstacle so in the early stages a dog should be sitting on one side of the jump with the handler on the opposite side, and the dog should be given the command 'over'. Jumping can be incorporated into all sorts of training situations – unseen retrieves, the 'get back' and hunting training.

As training progresses and an unseen retrieve is placed on the opposite side of a fence or wall from where the dog is being sent, the question often asked is what does the handler do to stop the dog hunting on this side of the boundary and to get it on to the other side to find the dummy or retrieve the game. In the early stages of training most young dogs will hunt up and down the boundary line unless they have 'winded' the dummy / game on the opposite side and have the ability to go over the obstacle to retrieve it. A more likely scenario will require the handler to 'stop' the dog and gain his attention at which point the command 'over' can then be given to encourage the dog to jump. Of course while it looks impressive when a dog leaves the handler and jumps the obstacle, picks the retrieve and returns with none, or little, additional handling, there are of course occasions when the dummy / game will not be on the other side so dogs must also not pre-empt a jump by assuming that what they have been sent for is on the other side.

Most accidents in the shooting field occur when dogs are trying to scale obstacles – either when being sent at speed for a retrieve or when returning and carrying game. A dog able to get over a solid, four feet jump at home carrying a one pound dummy is a far cry from sending it over a five feet stone wall or a wire fence while carrying a cock pheasant. So it's important to make sure a dog is confident about jumping and not just full of gung-ho rather than skill and judgement. The more opportunities you can give a dog to master his jumping skills – in terms of the type of obstacle –

the more proficient he will become and the safer he will be. It's especially important with youngsters not to allow them to get into a jumping situation they aren't prepared for and then struggle or scare themselves and lose confidence. Jumping can look very stylish and impressive but dogs must be capable and confident. No discussion about jumping would be complete without a mention of barbed wire. While there are those who are confident their dogs can – and do – jump fences topped with a strand of barbed wire, for me it's far too risky. Yes, some dogs cope with wire but apart from the ease with which wire can tear and cut a dog (and male dogs are even more at risk then bitches) wire is not always taut and straight and the sight of a dog in total panic caught up in barbed wire is not to be recommended. So avoid wire at all costs and even if you have to lift a dog over barbed wire, I'd much rather cope with a few jibes than risk a serious accident.

## Water work

The last thing you need is for water to be associated with panic and fear, so I can't stress enough how important it is to tackle water work with the same degree of control that you apply to other training. Try and locate a place you intend to introduce the dog to water that's quiet and where the water is shallow and shelves very slowly to avoid the youngster inadvertently getting out of its depth.

Any reluctance to enter can be overcome in the very early stages by tossing a stone into the shallows to make a splash and engender some encouragement – or even wading in yourself. Taking an older dog to bolster confidence is often very useful but it is essential that your older dog doesn't take off into the deep water for a swim or the youngster will follow and soon get out of its depth.

Don't forget that swimming is a very vigorous exercise for a dog; it has to learn to breathe differently, keep its legs active, be mindful of the direction it's travelling in, keep an eye and ear on you for instruction – and eventually retrieve the game. The aim is to steadily build up the dog's confidence in water so that the physical job of keeping afloat and not taking in gulps of water become automatic and then that it can concentrate on what it's being told to do.

Only by giving a youngster time to perfect the art of being in water, and emulating those synchronised swimmers instead of a paddle steamer

that's lost its way will you be able to start working on the level of control you have when working a dog in water.

Do not work from the premise that the dog will literally sink or swim and that if the former happens it will suffice to teach itself how to survive in water.

Once the young dog is clearly happy about being in water try a few retrieves from the shallows – always remembering that the dog *must* deliver the game and *not* stop to shake. Follow that with a few retrieves that entail a little swimming but not too much – and make sure the dummy isn't going to get washed further away than you intended by an unsuspecting current.

Try a few short retrieves from water that do not put the dog under too much pressure. Don't spoil things by doing too much retrieving directly from water or you will create a problem for yourself when needing to send the dog over water to retrieve game from the far bank. I try to get to this stage very quickly so that the dog doesn't become fixated on the assumption that the dummy is always floating somewhere on the surface.

A young dog has a lot to think about when training moves into water so take things steadily to retain control *(Photo: Anne Taylor)*

*Training the Working Labrador* • 197

So once again select a location for a marked retrieve where the 'swim' across to the bank isn't too far and that you are happy that your dog is well trained enough on land for you to 'push' him on over the water to the far side – most dogs will get half way across and even though it has hopefully marked the retrieve, will start spinning in the water as it looks for the dummy.

That's where you have to make sure the dog trusts you and will follow your instructions to keep on swimming until the bank is reached. If it has been well thrown the dummy should be easily seen and retrieved and the job must be accompanied by ample praise and encouragement! Focus more on getting a dog across water than retrieving from the water itself.

Of course as you extend the distances worked across water, just as on land, a dog may veer off the line on which he's been sent or may be distracted; using the stop whistle to attract the dog's attention and put him back on course is the way to deal with this. So it's vital that the dog is 'on the button' on the whistle on land before he's let loose on a larger expanse of water – always making allowance for the fact that stopping mid-swim isn't as easy to do with the same precision in the early stages of water training as stopping mid-gallop on land!

It may appear that training a dog in water means little more than duplicating the methods used on terra-firma but that's where most of the problems arise. In my experience everything goes up a gear when you put water into the equation, so start off in a situation in which you have ample control should things start to go wrong.

Working in water should become as normal for the dog as working on land. The key is to make sure the early stages are taken slowly with confidence-building as the primary aim. Even the most exuberant youngster can develop an aversion to water if anything untoward occurs because of over confidence on the part of the handler.

And in these times of extreme weather it's essential that dogs maintain a healthy respect for water. Any pheasants retrieved from a raging torrent of a river on a drive I was picking up on last season would easily have claimed the life of any unsteady dog that found the situation just too tempting.

It simply highlights the need for dogs to treat work on water with the same mind-set they apply to retrieves from land – a splash and a flutter of wet feathers should be as routine as the hard thud of a cock pheasant on dry ground.

## Introduction to shot

Fortunately gun shyness isn't common, but it does occur and is usually the result of the way a dog is managed – in terms of allowance not being made for a dog that is rather sensitive and in the way it is introduced to the sound of gunfire. It is to be hoped that introducing young dogs to the sound of gunfire is tackled at the appropriate time and that it has been dealt with before any form of dummy launcher is used because the 'crack' emitted by these devices can spook a dog enough to cause gun-shyness.

Starter pistols available from suppliers of gundog training equipment are ideal for introducing a dog to gunfire. It's important to make sure everything is going to work towards making this experience a 'positive' one so don't tag this on to a training session where the young dog has already had enough to exercise its brain and may well be in a heightened state of awareness. Choose a still day with no wind that can distort the sound. Let the dog have a few minutes freedom before you start the exercise. You will need an assistant to stand at least 40 yards away from you but in sight of the dog. I don't give any particular command to the dog, in fact I am quite happy if its concentration is on anything but the assistant with the pistol. And I don't want the pistol held high or to give any indication to the dog that the 'crack' is coming. With the assistant fully briefed and watchful of me and the dog I would usually allow the trigger to be pulled without my instigation and for the pistol to be held in a way that wasn't visible to the dog and not above head height. The dog will hear the sound and as soon as it happens I immediately give praise to dilute the whole experience. In most cases, provided the distance away from the dog was adequate, the dog should show little response

I would repeat this exercise daily but maintain the distance for at least the first three sessions and then gradually move closer. At any point at which the dog shows any distress, the distance should be increased. But making light of the occasion is the key to successfully getting a dog used to gunfire. As training progresses and combined with the dog's retrieving ability and his steadiness, a dummy can be thrown and a shot fired. Retrieves undertaken in this scenario are putting the dog well on the way to his ultimate goal as a working gundog and to moving towards a situation when a gun can be fired by his handler with the dog by his side, a situation we will deal with more fully in the final chapter.

Anne Taylor's successful show winner Ch Fabracken Remember Me is an accomplished working gundog *(Photo: Anne Taylor)*

Taking a young dog out on a shooting day as a means of providing his first experience of hearing gun fire can lead to serious problems. While they may not manifest themselves immediately, they can come back to haunt a handler who takes this short-cut approach. Likewise any notion of taking a dog close to a clay pigeon firing range or to a clay pigeon shooting competition is equally foolhardy. A dog needs to take in the experience of gunfire in a very methodical manner and not on the basis of assuming that 20 minutes of hearing gunshot will give him all the experience he needs. Even dogs that are sensitive by nature can be totally unaffected by the sound of gunfire, so it's all about how you introduce it. Likewise bold and confident dogs can just as easily become gun-shy if this part of their training isn't tackled properly.

# CHAPTER TWELVE

·

# The Real Thing

For those who shoot and own a Labrador simply as a gundog to perform a very basic 'no frills' job of retrieving game, much of the training advice given in this book may seem unnecessary. But to be fair to the dog, if not to the owner, a working Labrador that's expected to undertake even rudimentary gundog work deserves to know precisely what he is expected to do and how he's expected to do it. It is wrong to assume that apart from a few basic lessons in obedience, the best place for a young working gundog to learn his skills is 'on the job'.

Such an approach to training will not produce a dog that can function correctly and efficiently on a shooting day and simply leads to the badly behaved dogs that can often be seen making a mockery of their owners. A well-trained gundog that knows its job and will work in unison with its owner and not operate to its own agenda, is a joy to work with and a source of great satisfaction. If enough time is spent investing in a young dog's education and training in the first 12–15 months of its life, there will be years of enjoyment ahead.

But assuming you are confident that your dog's training has been successful and that you have achieved the all-important 'connection', that there is a rapport and understanding between you, that your dog listens to you, is steady and that you have the ability to stop him using the whistle,

the day will dawn when all the training on dummies and cold game can be left behind and he can to be introduced to the 'real world'.

This is the point at which all the hours spent training will be put to the test because no matter how well you think your dog is trained, a shooting day is a different bag of tricks – literally! Before you even consider shooting over the dog it's essential that the young dog adjusts to all the new temptations and distractions associated with shooting game.

The step between training on dummies and cold game and progressing to 'the real thing' is a big one and mustn't be rushed. All through our training we have been steadily using the building blocks stage by stage to enable the dog to gradually master its craft. And so the next stage must be taken a step at a time. Initially, on the first occasion the dog is introduced to a

A well-trained gundog knows its job and is an invaluable part of the shooting day situation where live game is being shot, the owner needs to be in a situation where he can maintain his full focus of attention on the dog – so leave the gun behind.

A spot of rabbit shooting or pigeon shooting is often considered a good introduction for a youngster being primed to begin work in the forth-coming season – although I have to say that rabbits can often be more of a wind-up for a youngster than sitting on the side-lines for half a day on partridges in September.

But the young dog has to move up and learn to cope with situations that are full of the unexpected. He has to learn to follow all the instructions he's been taught and apply the steadiness he's learned on dummies and 'dead' game, to an environment where the sights, sounds and smells are very different and enticingly disruptive to a young and inexperienced gundog. So take it very steady and think about what the dog's thinking. Get into his mind and imagine how all his senses are being bombarded and yet somewhere in there is constraint and know-how. These first occasions of introducing a young dog to game are hugely important and yet are often under valued in terms of their influence on the dog.

Rabbit shooting can be a really tough test for a youngster so be mindful of that. It must be approached as a means of compounding steadiness into the dog more than anything. Let the dog watch, listen and learn. Don't be in a rush to retrieve anything and when an opportunity does arise it must be to retrieve a rabbit he has not seen shot. The last thing a young dog must assume is that if it has been shot and the dog has marked it, then a retrieve will automatically follow. Fall into this trap and you have the makings of a running-in problem.

Stand back from the real action on a rabbit shooting day and just let the dog soak up the atmosphere to begin with. The excitement in the dog will no doubt be felt all the way up the lead but he has to learn his job. Nevertheless be aware of how tense he is or perhaps how relaxed he is. Don't be 'mute' as you stand with your dog but give him occasional words of encouragement – not too much or the reassurance can have the oppo-site effect. Just enough to keep the lines of communication open.

At some point in the day he must be allowed to retrieve a rabbit he hasn't seen shot, but use this as a training exercise and take very careful note of everything the dog does and how he responds to you. Just a couple of retrieves will be enough – and pile on the praise. This may not be his first day on the local shoot but it's just about as near to graduation day as you are going to get.

At the end of that experience the dog will not only have had a major test of his steadiness, he will have heard plenty of gunfire, seen other dogs working and been able to apply his scenting and hunting ability for the first time. Quite an achievement.

The progression from dummies and game to 'the real thing' is a big one and mustn't be rushed (*Photo: Anne Taylor*)

Without any doubt it is steadiness that is tested in these situations so don't try anything too brave and if you are out with friends rabbit shooting keep the young dog on a lead rather than risk him running in. For me rabbits are the ultimate in tail-bobbing temptation for a young dog so the last thing you want is for something to go wrong – such as the dog running in or chasing after a rabbit – and then having to deal with that. Yes it may well happen at some stage but at this early point in the progression of experience I like to keep on building up the positives and not sour the situation with a negative that needn't have happened.

Pigeon shooting can provide another good opportunity but be mindful of the dog being in a hide and hearing gunshot and also make sure he is only allowed a couple of birds and not permitted to 'hoover' up the bag. Of course pigeon feathers are very soft and some young dogs can have an issue with that so I like to have tried a youngster with a cold pigeon beforehand.

Build confidence in young dogs with marked 'no nonsense' retrieves *(Photo: Darren Wilkie)*

While a day on grouse may be worthwhile, a hot day in deep heather and very often in the heightened atmosphere of expectation among the Guns that tends to occur on many grouse days, I cannot say I am a big fan of putting young dogs on to grouse as an early live game experience.

Personally half a day being 'part of the furniture' on a partridge day or even a half-day in October on a small shoot where the dog can just mop up the occasional pheasant are hard to beat for exposing a youngster to what lies ahead of him as a working gundog. These days are ideal for simply putting the dog 'in the workplace'. It's somewhere he's never been before; he's an apprentice on his first day at work and he needs to take everything in before he tries anything himself. So with the permission of the keeper and/or the shoot captain and/or the person who organises the picking-up team, you should be able to position yourself at the relevant drives so that the dog can see and hear birds shot and see other dogs work.

How you progress this situation depends on the arrangement you have with the shoot but ideally you need to be able to find a quiet spot in between drives and let the dog have a simple unseen retrieve – either a bird that you know hasn't been picked or one that someone can place in some cover for you. This only needs to be a simple, no nonsense retrieve. The aim is to get the dog to undertake it successfully. For the dog the simplicity of the task is not important. For him this should complete the circle. Don't be in a rush to give a young dog too much work to begin with no matter how well he appears to be coping. A few half-days as a backroom boy with the picking-up team will serve you well. Even if you feel the dog has reacted well to his early shooting experiences don't suddenly abandon your training; there may well be some issues that the shooting days have highlighted and you will need to address these in some further training.

## Tests and trials

Field trials and working tests provide the two main levels of competitive gundog work. The majority of gundog clubs are affiliated to the Kennel Club which gives them the appropriate accreditation to stage tests and or trials if they are granted the necessary licence – all held under Kennel Club rules. Working tests are held during the spring and summer and are split into tests for puppies (dogs between six and eighteen months old), novice dogs and open dogs.

Field trial 'stakes' are staged from late summer on grouse and continue into the autumn and throughout the shooting season, although most retriever stakes are held prior to the New Year.

Working tests are extremely popular and offer a good opportunity to evaluate the working ability of young dogs. Most working tests are staged in a 'safari' style format where a set of different working situations and tests are arranged over the ground being used for the competition. Many working tests for open dogs – those with previous wins to their credit – are often conducted in a walked-up format mirroring that of a field trial. As yet there is no champion status for working test winners so no matter how well your dog fares in this sector of gundog competition he will never attain a title.

But it's a different situation in the highly competitive world of field trials where the Kennel Club awards the title of Field Trial Champion to dogs that have achieved the required wins (three days worth of Open stake wins). While field trials are very much the stamping ground of professional trainers and highly skilled handlers, they continue to attract entries and support from across the spectrum of owners who have a desire to compete.

Field trial entries are restricted by ballot so it's necessary to be a member of a good number of clubs and be prepared to travel long distances if you want to get the runs with your dog during the season.

Whether you are interested in working tests or field trials the best approach is to find out when and where a test or a trial is being held (there are about 170 Kennel Club affiliated gundog clubs in the UK) and to go along as a spectator (if it's a trial its appropriate to contact the secretary even though you only want to spectate). The occasion will give you an insight into how these events are run but also the standard of dogs competing and the level of experience they need to have.

## The big day – for real

But the day will eventually dawn when you will be shooting formally with the dog by your side or as a member of the picking up team. And on that day the moment will come when the first command is given and the dog is sent. It's a bit like a ship being launched for her maiden voyage – but is she seaworthy and is the captain in control?

No matter how many months have been spent training on dummies, no matter how 'in control' you felt you were when you went out rabbit

A true professional at work (*Photo: Peter Bates*)

shooting or the confidence you had in the shining pupil that emerged from the private lessons with a professional trainer, come the big day it's just you and the dog.

But as soon as that bird is cleanly picked and your dog is on its way back to present its first successful retrieve, there will undoubtedly be a sigh of relief. But don't overdo the amount of retrieving with a young dog – no matter how proficient you think he may be at the start. Far better to take things very steadily rather than rushing a raw youngster that may end up spending most of the season having to be bolted down to the peg or even left in the car!

It's good advice to 'work backwards' from the shoot day in terms of how to prepare your dog for his first proper day. It's easy to have everything planned down to the last detail in terms of kit and just assume that the dog will jump in the back of the car at home and then jump out ready and raring to go when you arrive at the shoot.

Make sure you put in a few worthwhile training sessions in the run-up to the first shoot day – but don't try anything too clever with the intention of trying to prepare him for the unexpected. Last minute cramming doesn't work with gundogs. Far better to go over some solid, basic work with the emphasis on steadiness and bolster his confidence.

It's important to maintain the dog's routine on the morning of the shoot day. So if he's used to a gallop and a modest feed stick with it. Particularly with a young dog on its first day it's unwise to over-load with a heavy meal before leaving home, but give him a meal that's well moistened – your dog will dehydrate during the journey and may well not drink as much as he should during the day.

Feed well ahead of your departure time and make sure the dog has emptied itself before you leave. It's a good idea to load your young dog into the car in plenty of time and not at the last minute. If departure is in a panic a young dog will pick up on the stress!

*Nothing goes un-noticed for the highly-tuned working Labrador*
*(Photo: Peter Bates)*

Give some thought to the shoot day you've selected as the occasion on which you will both sally forth as a working partnership. Make sure the keeper or shoot captain knows you have a new and inexperienced dog and choose a day that's likely to give you an opportunity to work your dog with confidence.

A dog making his debut at the peg shouldn't be expected to last all day. Choose selected drives if you can or just part of the day. As in training you want to give him every opportunity to succeed and not to fail.

Likewise with a picking-up dog. Choose your drives if you can and err on the side of training for steadiness – it will make that first retrieve even more satisfying.

At the first opportunity after arriving, and having undertaken the necessary courtesies, make sure you let your dog out of the car – on a lead of course – and give it the chance to relieve itself after the journey. I always give dogs a drink on arrival. Once the dog is settled back in the car – and has adequate ventilation – you can join fellow Guns or pickers-up for the pre-shoot gathering.

Whether Gun or part of the picking-up team, your young dog can be easily overawed by suddenly being hoisted out of the car into a sea of other dogs. So remain aware – especially with dogs or bitches that may be rather shy or equally a little 'bolshie' – that while you're enjoying the camaraderie of the occasion, your dog has been plunged into a canine hierarchy at ground level. Be mindful of this to avoid any untoward canine happenings that may thwart your day.

Guns with a new dog should pick the first retrieve with care. If there's a chance your dog is going to have its efforts undermined by the difficulty of the retrieve, or by having the bird snatched by another dog, it's far better to wait until the right opportunity presents itself. And the same goes for newcomers to the picking-up team. Far better to have one or two really good seen retrieves rather than drive after drive of frustrated whistle blowing and consummate failure.

Don't over-egg the pudding and if the morning has been a success, be happy to rest on your laurels and leave the dog in the car for the remainder of the day – making sure of course that the vehicle is secure and there is adequate ventilation.

I never put a wet dog back into a dog box without first giving a quick rub down with a towel – and for young dogs on their first day I believe it's

Focussed and committed to the job – another successful retrieve *(Photo: Sharon Rogers)*

OPPOSITE PAGE Every moment spent training will strengthen the bond of understanding between you and your dog

important to make the occasion less like an endurance test as possible. So dry the dog if it's wet, give it a light feed and a drink and leave it all to sink in while you repair to the shoot lunch.

A couple of good retrieves on the morning of the dog's first day will do for me but I also want to take home a dog that has enjoyed the experience and has used it as an invaluable part of its education. What I don't want is a dog that is cold, hungry and uncomfortable, has been over-worked, has under-achieved and felt totally overwhelmed by the occasion.

All of this isn't about pandering to working gundogs. It's about getting the best out of your dog by sensible and professional gundog management – as any experienced gundog man or woman will agree. So relish the first day with your new dog – but make sure you do as much as you can to ensure there are many more to follow.

# Index

# Acknowledgements

I am most grateful to all who have contributed and taken photographs for this book: Sharon Rogers (www.woodmistlabradors.co.uk), Anne Taylor (Fabracken), Peter Bates (Levenghyl), Darren Wilkie (Wilgunndi), Frank Toti and especially to my wife Anita for providing so many photographs and for all her hard work organising the illustrations and for her diligent final editing.

Jeremy Hunt